books designed with giving in mind

Pies & Cakes	Microwave Cooking	Natural Foods
Yogurt	Vegetable Cookbook	Chinese Vegetarian
The Ground Beef Cookbook	Kid's Arts and Crafts	The Jewish Cookbook
Cocktails & Hors d'Oeuvres	Bread Baking	Working Couples
Salads & Casseroles	The Crockery Pot Cookbook	Mexican
Kid's Party Book	Kid's Garden Book	Sunday Breakfast
Pressure Cooking	Classic Greek Cooking	Fisherman's Wharf Cookbook
Food Processor Cookbook	Low Carbohydrate Cookbook	Charcoal Cookbook
Peanuts & Popcorn	Kid's Cookbook	Ice Cream Cookbook
Kid's Pets Book	Italian	Blender Cookbook
Make It Ahead	Cheese Guide & Cookbook	The Wok, a Chinese Cookbook
French Cooking	Miller's German	Japanese Country
Soups & Stews	Quiche & Souffle	Fondue Cookbook
Crepes & Omelets	To My Daughter, With Love	

from nitty gritty productions

With Love to

Ron, who shares my journey, and

Richard, Jason and Michael, who brighten it.

The discovery of a new dish

does more for the happiness of mankind than the discovery of a star.

Brillat-Savarin, 1825

Yogurt

by
Susan Mintz

Illustrated by Mike Nelson

© Copyright 1978
Nitty Gritty Productions
Concord, California

A Nitty Gritty Book*
Published by
Nitty Gritty Productions
P.O. Box 5457
Concord, California 94524

*Nitty Gritty Books — Trademark
Owned by Nitty Gritty Productions
Concord, California

ISBN 0-911954-47-3
Library of Congress Catalog Card Number: 78-52807

Library of Congress Cataloging in Publication Data

Mintz, Susan.
    Yogurt.

    Includes index.
    1. Cookery (Yogurt)   I.   Title.
TX759.M56   641.6'7' 146   78-52807
ISBN 0-911954-47-3

TABLE OF CONTENTS

INTRODUCTION

Although acclaimed as the new food discovery of the decade, yogurt has been enjoyed for thousands of years.

The Bible refers to its healthful attributes. Religious scholars believe that yogurt is what was promised in the land "flowing with milk and honey." Abraham is said to have been a lifelong devotee of this "food of the gods" after an angel whispered to him the secret of its creation. Obviously, he knew a good thing when he heard it, as he lived to be a virile 175 years of age!

Yogurt is believed to have originated in Turkey. Legend has it that a nomad, trekking across the desert, tucked some milk away in a goatskin bag, slung it across the back of his camel, and traveled on. When he opened the bag hours later, he found his liquid refreshment transformed into a thick, tangy custard! Hot desert sun and the bacteria inside of the bag produced the ideal conditions to make the first yogurt. It soon became a staple in the diets of nomads who carried their yogurt with them as they migrated and settled throughout the Middle East, Central Asia and Southern Europe.

Yogurt reached Western Europe in the 1500's, again by a fluke of fate. A famous vignette tells of the seriously ailing French Emperor Francois I rapidly fading from an incurable intestinal disease. His illustrious court physicians could not save him. He sought help from an ancient Jewish healer, in far-away Constantinople, who was reputed to possess a magical cure. The doctor journeyed to Paris and concocted his special elixir for Francois who miraculously regained his strength and vitality. The mystical potion was none other than goat's milk yogurt! So enamoured of yogurt was Francois that he proclaimed it the milk of eternal life!

Eternal life was also what yogurt seemed to promise to Ilya Metchnikoff, a Nobel bacteriologist at the Pasteur Institute. While seeking the key to long life, Metchnikoff traveled to Bulgaria in the early 1900's to study the centenarians thriving there. He concluded that their longevity was due to the copious quantities of yogurt they consumed. He identified and isolated two strains of bacilli which convert milk to yogurt. Although his theories regarding yogurt and longevity were not proven, Metchnikoff's discovery of the bacteria opened the door for commercial production and distribution of yogurt. It was only a few years later that yogurt arrived in North America, where it has gained a place in the hearts and diets of millions of Americans.

YOGURT AND GOOD HEALTH

Yogurt is considered a miracle food by many, able to cure a myriad of human ailments. Although some claims regarding its merits are questioned, several healthful qualities of yogurt are widely accepted.

As a milk product, yogurt is a rich source of protein and essential vitamins and minerals. The protein of yogurt is more readily digested and better tolerated than the protein in milk. Yogurt is particularly ideal for those with sensitive digestive systems, including young children and elderly adults. During the yogurt-making process, the bacteria which convert milk to yogurt "predigest" (break down) the milk protein so that it is more quickly and easily assimilated by the body. These bacteria then work busily within the intestinal tract to inhibit growth of illness-causing bacteria and to maintain a healthy distribution of the beneficial bacteria needed for good digestion. If during an illness it is necessary to take antibiotics, often the antibiotics destroy the good intestinal bacteria along with the bad. Including yogurt in the diet during this time helps to restore the appropriate intestinal balance of the vital, beneficial bacteria. These same friendly bacteria seem to facilitate the availability and absorption of minerals and are widely-believed to aid in the synthesis of important B-vitamins.

MAKING YOUR OWN YOGURT

Making your own homemade yogurt is easy, economical, and—fun! Any kind of milk can be used to make yogurt—nonfat, lowfat and whole milk, dry milk, evaporated or condensed milk, and even soy milk. Add a yogurt culture, incubate the mixture in a warm place, and *voila!* you can enjoy your own fresh, homemade yogurt!

There are many advantages to making your own yogurt. The flavor of newly-made yogurt is far better than the flavor of commercial yogurt. You will be confident that your yogurt is free from additives and made from only the purest ingredients. You can control the number of calories contained in your yogurt. And, yogurt is very inexpensive to make at home. After you have made your first quart, you will have fresh starter available for subsequent batches. Your only cost then will be the quart of milk, currently just 1/3 the price of a quart of ready-made yogurt!

Simple, convenient units are now available for incubating the milk. However, yogurt has been made for centuries without the assistance of modern technology! Several methods for incubating yogurt make use of things you have already handy in your home. See Incubation Methods, page 12.

MAKING YOGURT —
GENERAL INFORMATION

EQUIPMENT — All utensils, pots, pans, yogurt cups and containers must be cleaned meticulously before you begin. Contamination of any of these can cause poor results in the taste or quality of your yogurt, or even complete failure of the milk to coagulate. Do not use aluminum pots or pans for heating or incubating the milk. Use glass, stainless steel, or enameled pots.

TEMPERATURE — Temperature is critical throughout the entire yogurt-making process. Milk should be heated to just barely boiling and then cooled to 110-115°F. before the culture is added. The milk is heated to destroy any foreign bacteria which might overpower or interfere with the action of the yogurt bacilli. Cooling to 110-115°F. puts the milk at the ideal temperature to introduce the yogurt culture. If the milk temperature drops below 90°F., the bacteria will be inactivated. If it is 120° or above, they will be destroyed by the heat. A thermometer, while not essential, is most helpful at this stage. A yogurt thermometer is usually included with the commercial yogurt makers, or one can be purchased separately. If you do not have a thermometer, test the temperature of the milk by

5

placing a few drops on your wrist. It should feel comfortably warm, *not hot.*

The starter containing the culture should be at room temperature before it is added to the cooled milk. If the milk is at the proper temperature, but the starter is removed from the refrigerator just before use, the temperature of the total mixture may be lowered so much during the mixing that it will take considerably longer for the milk to coagulate.

Before using, warm the containers which will hold the milk during incubation. This will help maintain the milk mixture at its ideal temperature. You can rinse the jars or pots with warm water, or put them in the oven near the pilot light (except plastic containers) to keep them warmed while you are preparing the milk. Or, put them in your dishwasher for a few minutes on the drying cycle. If you are using a commercial yogurt maker, it is easiest to place the clean jars into the unit, cover it, plug it in, and preheat them there. They will warm to the incubation temperature of the unit, and your mixture will sustain its proper temperature when it is poured into the jars.

Yogurt can be incubated successfully from 105-120°F. However, the action of the culture is slowed down when the temperature is as low as 105 degrees, and it will take longer for the yogurt to incubate. On the other hand, if the incubation temperature is too close to 120 degrees, there is the risk of destroying the bacilli. The higher temperature also tends to create a yogurt that has a tough texture with a very acidic flavor. Ideal incubation temperature is 110-115°F.

STARTER — Starter is the small amount of yogurt, containing the active yogurt bacilli, which is introduced into milk to cause it to coagulate and be transformed into yogurt. Starter is the *key* to good yogurt! Find a yogurt with a flavor and tang balance that you like, and use it for your first starter. It may be a fresh, dairy yogurt or one you find in a specialty restaurant or ethnic food store which makes its own yogurt. The yogurt which you use for your starter should be *very* fresh to accurately reproduce the same flavor in your homemade yogurt. Starter which is old will take longer to incubate and may distort the flavor of your yogurt. Be sure to use only yogurt in which the milk has been pasteurized *before* the yogurt culture has been added. Pasteurizing after the yogurt has been made (as is done with some commercial yogurts) kills the bacteria and stops their beneficial action. This type of yogurt is ineffective as a starter.

The starter should be at room temperature when it is added to the cooled milk. It must be thoroughly blended with the milk in order to achieve an even-textured yogurt. In a small dish, mix the starter with about 1/2 cup of the cooled milk until smoothly blended. Add the mixture to the pot of milk and blend. Or, *gently* whisk the starter alone into the pot of milk. Do not vigorously beat it in. The tranquility of the bacteria will be disturbed, and you may be disappointed with the results. Merely stirring starter into the milk with a spoon does not usually distribute the culture evenly.

Every 3 to 4 weeks make your yogurt with a newly-purchased fresh starter. As it ages, starter gradually becomes less effective, slower to make yogurt, and less true to the flavor that you have enjoyed.

TANG VARIATION — A main benefit of making your own yogurt is the ability to control and vary the flavor and degree of tang that your yogurt develops. You may want to make a mild-flavored yogurt for use with fruits or as a dessert base and then create a zestier yogurt for flavoring vegetables, salads or cooked dishes. Generally, a yogurt becomes more tart the longer it is incubated. Incubate the milk mixture for a shorter period of time (3 to 6 hours), and you will have a sweeter, milder yogurt. For an even sweeter yogurt, add a tablespoon or two of honey to the milk before heating.

The strain of bacteria which is used in the culture affects the taste and tang. There are two strains of bacteria that are used most often to make yogurt commercially—*Lactobacillus bulgaricus* and *Streptococcus thermophilus.* Sometimes these are supplemented with the addition of *Lactobacillus acidophilus* culture, reputed to be one of the most beneficial of the strains. Experiment with a dry culture from a different strain or combination of strains of bacteria for flavor variations in your homemade yogurt. Dry cultures take several hours more incubation time initially, even up to 24 hours. After you have made your first quart of yogurt from the dried culture, you will have a ready-made fresh starter for your next batch and the timing will be shorter. Dried cultures in the unopened package will keep several months, even longer if refrigerated or frozen. If you are camping or traveling to an area where fresh yogurt is unavailable, take along a package of the dried culture. You can make and enjoy your own fresh yogurt whenever and wherever you wish!

TIMING — Several variables affect the timing in making yogurt. These include the particular starter and its age, the freshness of the milk, the temperature and constancy of temperature maintained by the incubating method used. Even small temperature variations affect the length of time it will take for the milk to coagulate. Generally, if the starter and milk are fresh and the correct temperatures have been used, after 3 to 4 hours the milk will have begun to solidify. It is not necessary to wait until the yogurt is of a very firm custard consistency to interrupt the incubation. After a few hours, *gently* tip the yogurt container or cup to see if it has begun to thicken. If it has reached a soft-custard stage, you may refrigerate it at that point. The yogurt will continue to thicken as it chills, but it will not become more tangy. If you want a more tart yogurt, incubate it longer. Some methods of incubation will require a longer incubation period. With these methods check the yogurt after a few hours to see how far along it is. After you have made your own yogurt a couple of times, you will learn to gauge what stage it has reached in the process and approximately how much longer it will take to thicken.

INCUBATION METHODS

Incubate the prepared milk in any covered glass, ceramic or stainless steel container. Use jars, bowls, casserole dishes or pots. If lids or tops are not available, cover the container tightly with foil. Timing will vary with each method. When milk has congealed, chill yogurt until firm in the incubating container. You can then transfer the yogurt to other dishes for serving or storing.

ELECTRIC YOGURT MAKERS — Electric yogurt makers automatically maintain a constant incubation temperature. Most are designed to incubate yogurt in small glass jars provided with the unit and are inexpensive to operate. Their initial cost is quickly recovered from savings gained by making yogurt at home.

OVEN — Yogurt can be incubated very successfully by the warmth of the pilot light in a gas oven. Place the covered container of prepared milk on a rack in the top half of the oven. On a rack directly below, place a large, flat baking pan filled with boiling water. This will help to sustain the heat of the milk at the beginning of the incubation process. In an electric oven, turn the thermostat to the lowest possible setting. If the oven is still too hot, leave the door ajar while incubating the yogurt. Oven incubation is the easiest method to use for making large quantities of yogurt.

ELECTRIC SKILLET — Fill skillet about 2/3 full with water. Turn thermostat to lowest setting. Test water with thermometer until you find the setting which will maintain the temperature at 110-115°F. Place covered container of prepared milk into the warmed water. Cover skillet. Incubate several hours.

THERMOS — Pour hot water into wide-mouth thermos. Set aside while preparing milk. Empty thermos. Pour in milk mixture. Cap thermos. Incubate.

INSULATED FOAM FOOD CHEST — Pour prepared milk into container. Cover. Wrap with warm towel (warm the towel briefly in clothes dryer, drying cycle of dishwasher or in the sun). Place in foam chest. Cover chest. Incubate.

THERMAL BLANKET — Pour prepared milk into container. Cover. Wrap carefully in a thermal blanket. Set in a warm place. Incubate overnight.

YOGURT-MAKING TIPS

Rinse the pot or pan in cold water before you put the milk in to heat. This will make cleaning the pot afterward much easier!

Watch the milk carefully so that it doesn't scorch as it is heating. Even the slightest scorching on the bottom of the pot will affect the quality of the yogurt adversely and give it an unpleasant taste.

When the heated milk has cooled, remove the film which forms on the top before adding the starter. The film won't mix into the milk and will disrupt the yogurt-making process.

Don't add more than the amount of starter indicated in the recipes. It takes *very little* to begin the bacterial action. More starter results in crowding of the bacteria and an uneven, lumpy texture. The final flavor may be too acidic.

Put your yogurt maker or container in a place where it won't be jostled about during incubation. The bacteria have a distinct aversion to be disturbed and may just decide to quit working! Or, they may show their displeasure by producing a lumpy yogurt, or simply take longer to do their job.

Occasionally, after the yogurt is chilled and ready to eat, you will notice a watery liquid on top. This is whey and should be poured off. If it is stirred into the yogurt, the yogurt will thin out and may not regain its thicker consistency.

Save a small amount of yogurt each time to use as a starter for your next batch. After 3 to 4 weeks if your yogurt begins to lose the quality of taste that you like, begin again with a new, fresh starter either purchased or made from a dry culture.

Yogurt Maker

BASIC YOGURTS

NONFAT MILK YOGURT (0-1% Fat) — Nonfat milk is used for making a yogurt that is low in calories without the butterfat cholesterol of whole milk. A tasty yogurt can be made using 1 quart nonfat milk and 1 heaping tablespoon starter. For a yogurt with a more stable and creamier consistency, use the following recipe. Mix 1 quart nonfat milk with 1/4 to 1/3 cup dry nonfat milk powder. Heat to just boiling. Cool to 110-115°F. Add 1 heaping tablespoon starter. Incubate. This yogurt contains the fewest calories and has a slightly tart flavor.

    Calories per cup —   plain, 90   dry milk added, 150-170

LOWFAT MILK YOGURT (2% Fat) — Lowfat milk yields a yogurt of thick, creamy consistency which exchanges very nicely with whole milk in most recipes. It has fewer calories per cup than whole milk yogurt and a reduced butterfat content. Use 1 quart lowfat milk to 1 heaping tablespoon starter. For a slightly thicker yogurt, add 2 to 4 tablespoons dry nonfat milk powder to the milk before heating. The method is the same as for nonfat milk yogurt. Lowfat milk yogurt has a well-balanced, tangy flavor.

    Calories per cup —   plain, 120   dry milk added, 150-180

WHOLE MILK YOGURT (3.5% Fat) — Whole milk yogurt is more mellow than nonfat or lowfat milk yogurts, with a rich and creamy consistency. Use 1 quart milk to 1 heaping tablespoon starter. For a thicker yogurt, add 2 to 4 tablespoons dry nonfat milk powder to the milk before heating.

Calories per cup —   plain, 150   dry milk added, 180-210

LIGHT CREAM YOGURT (Half and Half) — This is the luxury yogurt. When calories definitely do not count, try this one! Cream yogurt is *very* thick with the consistency of sour cream. It is delicious—creamy, with just a hint of tang. No dry milk thickener is required. Simply use 1 quart half and half to 1 heaping tablespoon yogurt. This yogurt is a taste twin to the highly-prized French *creme fraiche* and is exquisite with fresh fruit and berries.

DRY MILK YOGURT — Yogurt made solely with dry nonfat milk powder is very similar to regular nonfat milk yogurt in taste and consistency. Its advantage is in its convenience. Equipped with dry milk powder and a dry culture, you can make yogurt anywhere! Reconstitute a quart of milk according to proportions indicated on the package, using boiling water. Dissolve an additional 1/4 to 1/3 cup milk powder in the hot milk. Cool to 110-115°F. Add 1 heaping tablespoon starter. Incubate.

EVAPORATED MILK YOGURT — Evaporated milk produces a rich, creamy yogurt. Use 1 can (13-1/2 ozs.) evaporated milk, 2-1/4 cups hot water, and 1/3 cup nonfat milk powder. Cool to 110-115°F. Add 1 heaping tablespoon starter. Incubate. Evaporated milk has been sterilized in the canning process. It does not need to be boiled.

DRAINED YOGURT — Drained yogurt is useful for making some dips, dressings or flavored yogurts if a thicker consistency is desired. When yogurt is drained in cheesecloth for 1 to 2 hours, it loses some of the whey and becomes thicker. Use the same method as for Yogurt Cheese, page 26, but drain the yogurt only an hour or two.

FRUIT YOGURTS

Fruit yogurts are fresher-tasting when the fruit is added after the yogurt is made. The very best fruit yogurts can be made quickly and easily by adapting the frozen yogurt recipes in this book, pages 167-179. The flavor of these yogurts is excellent, more natural and far richer than the commercial flavored yogurts.

Use the ingredients and proportions suggested in the frozen yogurt recipes, but make two changes.

1) Reduce the gelatin to 1 teaspoon per 2 cups of yogurt-fruit mixture. This will thicken the yogurt, but will not give it an overly-jelled consistency.

2) Chill the mixture for several hours. Do not freeze it.

FRUITED DRAINED YOGURT — Fold chopped, fresh fruit into yogurt that has been drained in cheesecloth (see page 18) for 1 to 2 hours. Chill.

FLAVORED YOGURTS

Make the basic yogurt (see page 16) with 1 quart milk, 1/4 to 1/3 cup dry non-fat milk, and 1 tablespoon starter. Add the flavoring. Incubate.

SWEETENED YOGURT — Add 1/4 to 1/3 cup sugar or 2 to 4 tablespoons honey to milk while it is heating. This yogurt makes a nice base for fruit yogurts if you like an added touch of sweetness. For variation, add 1 teaspoon cinnamon. Or, try 1/4 cup brown sugar with 1 teaspoon Mapleine.

VANILLA YOGURT — Add 1 tablespoon vanilla to 1 quart sweetened milk mixture before incubating. This also is a good base for fruit yogurts. Try any of the other pure flavoring extracts in place of vanilla. Use 1 teaspoon orange or lemon extract, or 3/4 teaspoon almond extract, or 1/2 teaspoon mint extract.

SWISS-STYLE FRUIT YOGURT — Add 1/2 to 1 cup pureed fresh, frozen (defrosted) or canned fruit to cooled milk mixture. Or, stir 1/2 cup preserves into cooled milk.

"FRUIT-AT-THE-BOTTOM" YOGURT — Spoon 2 tablespoons chopped fresh fruit, preserves, applesauce, strained baby fruit, or canned fruit pie filling into the bottom of individual yogurt cups. Gently pour in cooled milk mixture (sweetened, if desired).

JUICE YOGURTS — Heat slowly to 115°F., 2 cups evaporated milk, 2 cups apple juice, 2 tablespoons honey, 1 cinnamon stick, and 2 cloves. Remove spices. Add 1 tablespoon starter. Incubate. Or, use 2 cups evaporated milk, 2 cups V-8 juice, 1/2 teaspoon onion powder, 1/2 teaspoon celery salt, 1 tablespoon tomato paste, and 1 tablespoon starter.

SYRUP YOGURTS — Add 1/2 cup flavoring syrup to milk mixture before incubating. Use chocolate, maple or fruit syrup, or 3/4 cup Kern's Cream of Coconut.

POWDERED FLAVORINGS — Mix a small amount of milk into 6 tablespoons powdered flavoring to dissolve. Blend in yogurt. Add to pot of cooled milk. Incubate. Try instant cocoa or coffee mixes.

THE ART OF COOKING WITH YOGURT

Always bring yogurt to room temperature before combining with hot foods.

Before measuring yogurt, stir it gently until well-blended and creamy.

Yogurt, like all milk products, is sensitive to heat. Cook yogurt *briefly* and over *low heat* only, or it will separate and curdle. *Never* bring foods containing yogurt to a boil.

Yogurt should not be added to a boiling or very hot mixture. If mixture is too hot, let it cool slightly before combining with room temperature yogurt.

To combine yogurt with hot foods, gradually stir a few tablespoons of the hot mixture into the yogurt. *Slowly,* add warmed yogurt to hot mixture, stirring.

When possible, add yogurt to hot foods near the end of cooking time or just before serving. This will reduce the chance of the yogurt curdling.

If temperature of heated foods is maintained below 120°F., yogurt bacilli will remain alive and will retain their beneficial qualities. Above 120°F. they will be destroyed, but the flavor and texture of the food will continue to be enhanced by the addition of the yogurt.

In hot sauces, the addition of flour, cornstarch or arrowroot to the yogurt may help prevent separation or thinning of the sauce. Mix flour with small amount of water to moisten, stir into yogurt, combine with hot ingredients. Or, before adding yogurt, incorporate flour into sauce. Try 1 to 2 tablespoons flour per cup yogurt.

In baking, substitute yogurt for milk, buttermilk or sour cream. Be sure to include 1/2 teaspoon baking soda for each cup of yogurt used in the recipe.

If yogurt thins out too much when mixing salad dressings, dips or cold soups, chill mixture for an hour or two, and it will re-thicken.

APPETIZERS

Yogurt is a perfect addition to the abundant array of foods served as hors d'oeuvres. Its zesty flavor provides a welcome appetite stimulant. Plain yogurt, drained yogurt and yogurt cheese all can be used inventively to prepare savory delicacies to tease the palate and tempt the appetite.

Use yogurt alone or combined with cottage cheese, ricotta or Neufchatel cheese for a rich-tasting, low-calorie dip base to which you may add your favorite seasonings. Hollow out cherry tomatoes, fill with yogurt, and garnish with smoked oysters. For a quick, elegant first course, season yogurt with minced shallots or green onions, spoon into avocado halves, and top with red caviar.

When drained overnight, yogurt becomes a creamy cheese to which spices, herbs, nuts and fruits can be added for appetizer spreads and sandwich fillings. Mushroom caps are delicious when stuffed with a mixture of yogurt cheese, Parmesan cheese and a dash of tarragon, topped with finely-chopped almonds and broiled until lightly browned.

Think "yogurt!" when you are making appetizers, and you will discover new flavor variations for familiar favorites—and, with fewer calories!

YOGURT CHEESE

Yogurt cheese is very similar in taste and texture to cream cheese, but without the calories! Drain yogurt overnight, and in the morning you will find a ball of creamy cheese ready to be used for tasty appetizer spreads or sandwich fillings. This is an excellent way to use leftover or aging yogurt. The older the yogurt, the tangier the cheese. Some commercial yogurts are not satisfactory for making yogurt cheese. They are overly-stabilized, and the whey may not drain off fully. Best results will be achieved with homemade yogurt or a dairy yogurt not highly thickened.

TO MAKE YOGURT CHEESE — Fold a large piece of cheesecloth into 2 or 3 thicknesses. Lay it across a bowl, moisten it with water. Pour yogurt into center of cheesecloth. Gather ends together and tighten with a thick rubber band, forming a bag-like container. Hang bag from kitchen faucet, or place in a footed colander, to drain into sink overnight. The whey will drain from the yogurt, leaving a ball of soft cheese. Mix with seasonings and chill. Spread on buttered toast fingers, cocktail breads or crackers, apple or pear slices. Yogurt cheese is also good served plain, salted or sugared with fresh fruits and vegetables.

YOGURT CHEESE SPREADS

To 1 cup yogurt cheese add any of the following combinations:

2 tablespoons each minced parsley and chives, 1 teaspoon oregano, basil or tarragon, 1/4 cup mayonnaise.

1/3 cup flaked coconut, 1/4 cup each finely-chopped pecans and dates, 2 tablespoons honey, 1/4 teaspoon curry powder, 1/8 teaspoon powdered ginger.

1 cup ground ham, 1/3 cup finely-chopped raisins, 2 teaspooons prepared mustard, 2 tablespoons mayonnaise, 1 tablespoon honey, 1/4 teaspoon ground cloves.

1-1/2 cups shredded cheddar cheese, 1/2 cup applesauce, 2 tablespoons honey, 1/4 teaspoon dry mustard, 1/2 teaspoon allspice, 1/4 teaspoon cinnamon, 1 to 2 tablespoons port (optional).

YOGURT CHEESE SPREADS continued

1/2 cup jam, jelly or fruit butter. A large variety of fruit butters is available in health food stores.

1/2 cup *each* finely-chopped dates and walnuts, 1 tablespoon honey, 1/2 teaspoon cinnamon. Variation — Chill. Shape into 3/4-inch balls. Roll in toasted coconut.

1/2 cup finely-crumbled bacon, 2 tablespoons bleu cheese, 2 tablespoons minced chives, 1 teaspoon tarragon, 2 tablespoons mayonnaise. Variation — Chill. Form into 3/4-inch balls. Roll in ground cashews.

1 can (4-1/2 ozs.) cocktail shrimp, drained and minced, 2 tablespoons minced chives, 2 tablespoons mayonnaise, 1/2 teaspoon dried dill, 1/2 teaspoon mustard, 1/2 teaspoon toasted sesame oil.

1/4 cup *each* dried figs or dates, raisins and salted peanuts, 2 tablespoons orange marmalade — all finely chopped. Add dash cinnamon.

CHICKEN-CHUTNEY BALLS

1/2 cup yogurt cheese, page 26
1/4 cup mayonnaise
1 cup ground cooked chicken
1/2 cup finely-chopped roasted cashews
3 tbs. chopped chutney
1 tsp. curry powder
1 tbs. honey
1/2 cup flaked coconut

Cream together cheese and mayonnaise. Combine with chicken, cashews, chutney, curry and honey. Form into 1-inch balls. Roll in coconut. Chill. Serve with cocktail picks. Makes 2 dozen 1-inch balls.

RIPE OLIVE DIP

2 cans (4-1/4 ozs. ea.) Lindsay chopped black olives
1 cup drained yogurt, page 18
8 ozs. cream cheese
3 tbs. minced parsley
2 tbs. minced shallots
1/2 tsp. dried basil, crushed

Drain olives thoroughly. Cream together yogurt and cheese. Fold in olives and remaining ingredients. Chill. Serve with raw vegetables or cocktail crackers.

SPICY PLUM DIP

1 cup drained yogurt, page 18   2 tbs. bottled barbecue sauce
1/2 cup plum jam   1/2 tsp. cinnamon

Combine ingredients. Use as dip for cocktail franks or meatballs.

ARTICHOKE DIP

1 cup drained yogurt, page 18
1/2 cup cottage cheese
1 jar (6 ozs.) marinated artichokes
2 tbs. minced shallots
1/2 tsp. dried oregano leaves
1/2 tsp. freshly-ground pepper

Combine ingredients in blender. Chill. Serve with corn chips. Makes 2 cups.

DEVILED HAM DIP

1 cup yogurt
1 can (4-1/2 ozs.) deviled ham
2 tbs. bottled chili sauce

2 tbs. minced chives
2 tsp. sweet pickle relish
1/2 tsp. prepared horseradish

Combine ingredients. Chill. Serve with cocktail crackers. Makes 1-3/4 cups.

CLAM DIP

1 can (6-1/2 ozs.) minced clams
1/2 cup drained yogurt, page 18
4 ozs. cream cheese
1 tbs. chopped chives
1 tbs. lemon juice
1/2 tsp. seasoned salt
1/4 tsp. dried thyme, crushed
2 to 3 drops Tabasco sauce
1 tsp. tomato paste (optional)

   Drain and finely chop clams. Cream together yogurt and cheese. Combine with clams and remaining ingredients. Chill. Serve with potato chips or wheat crackers. Makes 1-1/4 cups.

DILL DIP

Arrange a colorful selection of crisp raw vegetables in a bowl of chipped ice to serve with this dip.

2 tsp. instant dried onion
1/4 cup water
2 cups yogurt
1/2 cup mayonnaise

2 tbs. dried parsley flakes
4 tsp. dried dill weed
1-1/4 tsp. Lawry's seasoned salt
1 tsp. lemon juice

Soften onion in water. Set aside 10 minutes. Combine all ingredients. Chill 2 to 3 hours. Serve with raw vegetables or potato chips. Makes about 3 cups.

SUGGESTED VEGETABLES — carrot sticks, celery sticks, cauliflowerettes, zucchini slices, cherry tomatoes, cucumber slices, eggplant fingers, mushrooms, radishes, broccoli buds, whole green beans, sweet red pepper strips, or cooked artichoke leaves.

SPINACH-MUSHROOM DIP

1 pkg. (10 ozs.) frozen, chopped spinach
2 cups yogurt
1 cup chopped fresh mushrooms
4 strips cooked bacon, crumbled
1 tbs. lemon juice
1 clove *finely*-minced garlic
1 tsp. tarragon
1 tsp. grated orange zest
1 tsp. sugar
1 tsp. seasoned salt
1/2 tsp. freshly-ground pepper

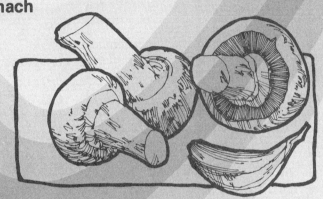

   Cook spinach according to package directions. Drain. Press out *all* of liquid. Combine with remaining ingredients. Chill 2 hours. Serve with sesame crackers or cocktail rye bread. Makes 4 cups.

CHINESE HOISIN CHICKEN

This recipe enlarges easily for a buffet side dish or an hors d'oeuvre served with crackers.

3 half chicken breasts
butter
salt and pepper
1/2 cup yogurt
1 tbs. hoisin sauce

1 tbs. soy sauce
1 tbs. sugar
1 tsp. toasted sesame oil
1/4 cup sliced green onion tops
1 to 2 tbs. toasted sesame seed

Cut chicken into thin strips. Saute in sizzling butter 1 to 2 minutes or until no longer pink. Salt and pepper to taste. Cool. Combine yogurt, hoisin, soy and sugar. Lightly toss together chicken, onions and sauce. Garnish with toasted sesame seed. Makes 4 to 6 appetizer servings.

HERRING APPETIZER

1 jar (6 ozs.) herring snacks in wine
1 small apple
1 hard-cooked egg (optional)
1/2 small onion
2/3 cup yogurt
1 tbs. sugar
1 tsp. mustard seed
1/4 tsp. cinnamon
freshly-ground pepper to taste

Drain herring well. Chop herring with its onions. Chop apple and egg. Thinly slice onion. Combine herring, apple, egg, onion, yogurt, sugar, mustard seed, cinnamon and pepper. Chill several hours. Garnish with sliced apple. Serve with cocktail pumpernickel bread.

VARIATION — To serve as a first course, heap on lettuce leaves and garnish with drained, canned julienne beets and sliced apples.

COQUILLES SAINT JACQUES

1 lb. bay scallops
1 cup white wine
1 bay leaf
4 tbs. butter
3 tbs. minced shallots
1/2 lb. sliced fresh mushrooms
3 tbs. flour
1 cup reserved wine broth
1/4 cup hot milk
1/2 cup yogurt
2 egg yolks
1/4 tsp. Dijon-style mustard
1 tbs. minced parsley
salt and white pepper
1/2 cup grated Swiss or Gruyère cheese

Place scallops, wine and bay leaf in saucepan. Poach scallops gently over low heat 5 minutes. Drain well. Reserve liquid. Melt butter in saucepan. Saute shallots and mushrooms. Add flour and cook over low heat 2 minutes, stirring. Remove from heat. Blend in reserved wine broth and hot milk. Heat gently until thickened. In bowl, combine yogurt and egg yolks. Slowly stir hot sauce into yogurt. Season with mustard, salt and pepper. Fold in scallops and parsley. Spoon into buttered ramekins or baking shells. Sprinkle with grated cheese, dot with butter. Bake in 400°F. oven 15 to 20 minutes until lightly browned. Serve immediately. Makes 8 appetizers or 4 luncheon entrees.

BEVERAGES

Delicious beverages can be made with yogurt! Combine yogurt with fruits, vegetables or juices for beverages which can be served as an energizing snack, a light lunch, a quick wholesome breakfast, or an after-school treat. A yogurt libation is the ideal thirst-quenching cooler in the heat of midsummer.

The beauty of these beverages is that they can be prepared in seconds! Simply place the ingredients in the blender container, whirl until smooth, and pour into a tall, frosty glass for instant nutritious refreshment! For an extra boost of protein add an egg, some wheat germ or a few tablespoons of powdered Tiger's Milk.

BEVERAGES

Place the following combinations in blender container and whirl until smooth. Serve in tall glasses.

STRAWBERRY-BANANA — 2 cups sliced strawberries (fresh or frozen), 2 bananas, 1 cup yogurt, 1/2 cup milk, 2 tablespoons honey, dash cinnamon. Makes 3 servings.

SPICY APPLE — 1-1/2 cups apple juice, 2 cups yogurt, 1 peeled apple, 2 table-spoons brown sugar, 1/4 teaspoon allspice, 1/4 teaspoon cinnamon. Makes 3 to 4 servings.

TROPICAL CREAM — 1 cup diced papaya, 1 cup pineapple juice, 1 cup yogurt, 1/2 cup milk, 1/4 cup flaked coconut, 2 tablespoons lime juice, 2 tablespoons honey. Makes 3 to 4 servings.

CHOCOLATE-NUT — 1 cup yogurt, 1 cup milk, 1/2 cup peanut butter, 1/2 cup chocolate sauce. Makes 3 servings.

ORANGE-CRANICOT — 1 cup Cranicot juice, 1/2 cup orange juice, 1 cup yogurt, 1 tablespoon honey, 1/8 teaspoon cinnamon. Makes 2 to 3 servings.

SUMMER DELIGHT — 2 fresh peaches and 2 ripe apricots (peeled and pitted), 1 large banana, 2 cups milk, 1 cup yogurt, 1/4 teaspoon almond extract, dash allspice. Makes 4 to 5 servings.

AVOCADO-PINEAPPLE — 1 medium-sized, ripe avocado, 1 cup pineapple juice, 1-1/2 cups yogurt, 1/2 cup milk, 1 tablespoon honey, few mint leaves. Makes 3 to 4 servings.

BERRY-BERRY — 1 package (10 ozs.) frozen raspberries, 2 cups yogurt, 1 cup vanilla frozen yogurt, 2 tablespoons sugar, 1/4 teaspoon cinnamon. Makes 4 to 6 servings.

COCONUT — 1 cup yogurt, 1 cup milk, 1/2 cup flaked coconut, 1 tablespoon honey, 1/2 teaspoon almond extract. Makes 2 to 3 servings.

BEVERAGES continued

MINTY MELON — 2 cups diced cantaloupe, 1-1/2 cups yogurt, 3 tablespoons apple-mint jelly. Makes 2 to 3 servings.

ORANGE FROSTY — 2 cups orange frozen yogurt, 1-1/2 cups milk, 1 banana, freshly-grated nutmeg. Makes 3 to 4 servings.

DATE-NUT SHAKE — 1 cup yogurt, 1/2 cup milk, 1/2 cup chopped dates, 1/4 cup blanched almonds, 1 cup vanilla frozen yogurt, 1/4 teaspoon cinnamon. Makes 3 servings.

CREAMY NECTAR — 1 cup fruit nectar (apricot, guava, peach, coconut-pineapple, etc.), 1 cup yogurt, dash cinnamon or nutmeg. Makes 2 servings.

EAST INDIAN LASSI — 1 cup yogurt, 3 cups ice water, 1 teaspoon cumin seed, roasted, 1/2 teaspoon salt, dash cayenne pepper. Chill this traditional drink for several hours before serving. Makes 4 servings.

ORANGE-A-MATO — 1-1/2 cups tomato juice, 1 cup orange juice, 1/2 cup yogurt, 2 teaspoons sugar, 1/2 teaspoon seasoned salt, 1/2 teaspoon basil. Makes 3 servings.

APRICOT-MELON — 1 cup diced cantaloupe, 1 cup apricot nectar, 1/2 cup yogurt, 1/8 teaspoon cinnamon. Makes 2 servings.

CLAMATO — 1 can (6 ozs.) minced clams with juice, 1 cup V-8 juice, 1 cup yogurt, 1/2 teaspoon seasoned salt, 1/4 teaspoon oregano, 2 drops Tabasco, 1 tablespoon lemon juice. Makes 2 to 3 servings.

FRENCH PRUNE-APPLE — 1 carton (8 ozs.) French apple yogurt, 1 cup prune juice. Makes 2 servings.

GARDEN MEDLEY — 1 small carrot, 1 small stalk celery, 1 small green onion, 1/4 peeled cucumber, 1 cup V-8 juice, 1 cup yogurt, 1/2 teaspoon seasoned salt, 1 to 2 tablespoons lemon juice, 1 can (8 ozs.) crushed pineapple with juice, 1/2 teaspoon basil or oregano. Makes 3 to 5 servings.

SOUPS

From the robust soups of hard-working peasantry to the jellied madrilenes of cushioned royalty, soup has provided sustenance for every culture throughout history. It appears on today's tables as an appetizing prelude to the meal, a hearty, satisfying main dish, or a delightful dessert. The creamy tang of yogurt brings an exciting flavor dimension to all types of of hot and cold soup—fruit, vegetable, meat, fish or cheese. A bowl of icy-cold yogurt soup cheers the sagging spirit on a sizzling summer day. Hot yogurt soup, ladled steaming into mugs on a nippy winter evening, promises renewed vitality and comfort to the chilled body.

To make an easy, refreshing cold soup, combine equal parts yogurt and any fresh fruit in the blender, add a dash of spice and chill. For a picnic basket treat, pour the soup into a chilled thermos, and serve it in halved orange or grapefruit shells. Create new canned soup combinations with yogurt. Try 2 cans cream of oyster soup and 1 can tomato soup heated with 1 cup yogurt and a dash of basil, or, combine 1 can mushroom soup with 1/2 cup yogurt, lace with 1 tablespoon sherry and garnish with snipped, fresh dill. Yogurt can replace all or part of the water used to dilute condensed soups and enrich dehydrated soup mixes. A

47

quick vichysoisse can be made with 1 package (2-3/4 ozs.) of Knorr Leek Soup mix cooked with 2-1/2 cups water. When cool, fold in 1-1/2 cups yogurt and chill.

Cold soups should be *very* cold. Make them several hours before you intend to serve them. Chill serving dishes in the freezer for a few minutes before filling. Beaded moisture on a frosty tureen or bowl of cold soup adds to the icy illusion and cooling effect.

Serve your soups imaginatively and attractively. Use interesting and unusual containers. If you search your home, you will discover soup tureens in many disguises! Perhaps a large glass or crystal vase is just right—or an elegant wine decanter, a colorful plastic ice bucket, a whimsical cookie jar, a silver wine cooler, flower pots (without the holes in the bottom!), a giant brandy snifter, tea and coffee carafes, and, for a large crowd, a gaily-painted ceramic rumpot is perfect! Serve individual portions not only in soup bowls, but use champagne glasses, sherbet dishes, pottery mugs, parfait glasses, mini-flower pots, seafood cocktail dishes (put crushed ice in the liners for extra-cold soup), china cups with saucers or large-bowled wine glasses. Containers are everywhere just waiting to be filled with soup!

SADIE'S RUSSIAN BORSCHT

A family favorite—always cooked for us with lavish scoops of love!

4 large beets with leaves
2 to 3 lemons
1 tsp. salt
1/2 tsp. freshly-ground pepper
1 egg

3 cups yogurt
1 tbs. sugar
1 cucumber, peeled and diced
4 green onions with tops, sliced
5 hard-cooked eggs, chopped

Scrub beets well. Peel thinly and grate. Wash leaves well. Discard any that are bruised. Shred remaining leaves. Place beets and leaves in large pot. Add cold water to cover. Add juice of 1/2 lemon, salt and pepper. Bring to boil. Reduce heat, cook 8 to 10 minutes. Skim foam from top. Cool slightly. Beat egg in separate bowl. Slowly add 1 cup warm beet liquid to egg, whisking constantly. Return egg mixture to beets, stirring. Chill. Before serving, place yogurt in bowl, stir well. Add juice of 1 lemon and sugar. Fold in cucumber, onions and eggs. Stir into chilled beet mixture. Season to taste with salt, sugar or lemon juice. Top each serving with yogurt. Makes 8 to 10 servings.

CARROT-ORANGE SOUP

Subtle flavor hints of orange and dill bring carrots to a new peak of perfection in this cooling soup.

3 tbs. butter
1 lb. carrots, peeled and sliced
2 medium leeks, sliced (white only)
or 1 onion, sliced
1 tbs. sugar
2 cups chicken stock

1 tsp. dried dill
or 1 tbs. fresh dill
2 tbs. frozen orange concentrate
1 cup yogurt
salt and white pepper

Melt butter in skillet. Add sliced carrots and leeks. Sprinkle with sugar. Saute until leeks are translucent and soft. Do not brown. Add chicken stock and dill. Cover. Simmer gently until carrots are tender, about 15 minutes. Cool. Puree in blender. Stir in orange juice, then yogurt. Season to taste. Chill thoroughly. Garnish with yogurt and shredded fresh carrot or chopped chives. Makes 4 to 6 servings.

FRESH TOMATO SOUP

Pure essences of fragrant, sun-ripened tomatoes permeate this delectable, refreshing cold soup.

2 lbs. red, ripe tomatoes
2 green onions, including tops
2 cups yogurt
1 tbs. sugar
2 tsp. salt
1/2 tsp. dried oregano leaves, crushed
1/2 tsp. dried basil leaves, crushed

Place tomatoes in blender container. Blend until pureed. Sieve. Discard skin and seeds. Set aside puree. Slice onions very finely. Combine tomato puree, onions, yogurt, sugar, salt and herbs. Chill thoroughly. Serve with freshly-ground pepper to sprinkle on top. Makes 4 to 6 servings.

VARIATION — Before serving, add 1 cup shredded ham or cucumber.

51

CREAMY AVOCADO SOUP

2 cups mashed avocado
1 cup chicken broth
2 tbs. fresh lime juice
1/2 tsp. chili powder
2 tbs. minced onion
1/2 tsp. salt
1-1/2 cups yogurt
1 to 2 tbs. sherry
1 diced avocado
chopped chives
lime wedges

    Place mashed avocado, broth, lime juice, chili powder, onion, salt and yogurt in blender container. Cover. Blend on low speed until smooth. Add sherry. Correct seasoning to taste. Chill. Before serving, fold in one diced avocado. Garnish with chopped chives and lime wedges. Makes 4 to 6 servings.

MIDEAST CUCUMBER SOUP

Variants of this soup appear throughout the Middle Eastern countries and in Bulgaria, Yugoslavia and Rumania. In the Balkan countries it is called tarator soup, made with Bulgarian yogurt—reputed to be the best in the world.

2 cups yogurt	1 to 2 tbs. minced fresh mint
1 clove garlic	1/2 cup chopped walnuts
1 tbs. red wine vinegar	salt
2 medium cucumbers	freshly-ground pepper

Place yogurt, garlic, and vinegar in blender container. Blend until garlic pieces are no longer visible. Peel and halve cucumbers. Remove seeds with tip of spoon. Shred cucumbers. In bowl combine cucumbers, mint, nuts and yogurt mixture. Season with salt and pepper. Chill 1 to 2 hours. Garnish each serving with mint leaves and dust with freshly-ground pepper. Makes 4 servings.

CORN-CHILI CHOWDER

2 cups milk
1/2 cup shredded Monterey Jack cheese
4 slices bacon, diced
1 onion, chopped
1 medium zucchini, sliced
1/2 bay leaf
3 tbs. canned diced green chile
1 can (16 ozs.) creamed corn
1 cup yogurt
1 large, ripe tomato

Scald milk. Set aside to cool. Skim. Shred cheese. In large saucepan saute bacon until partially cooked. Add onion, zucchini and bay leaf. Continue sauteing until vegetables are tender and bacon is lightly browned. Remove bay leaf. Stir in chile. Add milk and corn. Before serving, add yogurt and cheese. Heat gently, stirring, until cheese melts. Peel, seed and chop tomato. Fold into chowder. Garnish each serving with crumbled bacon. Makes 4 to 6 servings.

CHEDDAR CHOWDER

4 cups (about 1 lb.) grated cheddar cheese
6 tbs. butter
1/2 cup finely-chopped carrots
1/2 cup finely-chopped celery
1/2 cup finely-chopped onion
1/2 cup finely-chopped green pepper
4 tbs. flour
4 cups homemade chicken stock
or 3 cans (10-3/4 ozs. ea.) canned broth
1 tsp. Dijon-style mustard
1 tsp. Worcestershire sauce
2 cups yogurt
2 to 3 tbs. white wine or sherry
2 cups diced, cooked potatoes

    Grate cheese. Set aside to bring to room temperature. Melt butter in top of 3-quart double boiler over direct heat. Add carrots, celery, onion and green pepper. Saute until soft but not browned, about 10 minutes. Sprinkle in flour. Stir well. Cook over very low heat 2 to 3 minutes. Slowly add broth, stirring constantly. Add mustard and Worcestershire. Continue to cook over low heat until slightly thickened. At this point, place top of double boiler over hot, not boiling, water. Add cheese in small amounts, heating just until cheese melts. Slowly stir in yogurt and wine. Do not overcook or cheese will become stringy or tough. Fold in cooked potatoes. Season to taste. Ladle into soup mugs. Serve with hot crusty French bread and crisp green salad. Makes 6 to 8 servings.

VARIATION — Add 2 cups leftover diced ham, turkey or chicken.

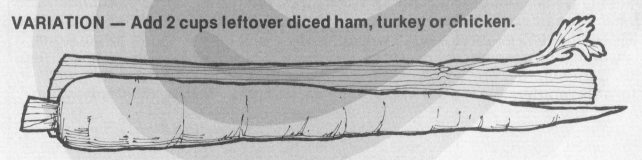

CLAM CHOWDER

3 cans (6-1/2 ozs. ea.) chopped clams
1/3 lb. diced bacon
1-1/2 cups chopped onion
2 large potatoes, pared and diced
bottled clam juice or water

1/2 tsp. dried thyme, crushed
1-1/2 cups yogurt
salt and pepper
butter pats

Drain clams, reserve liquid. In large saucepan, saute bacon over medium heat until translucent, about 10 minutes. Add onion. Continue to saute until onion is tender, not brown. Add potatoes, reserved clam liquid and enough additional juice or water to barely cover potatoes. Cover. Simmer until potatoes are tender, about 15 minutes. Liquid will cook down and be thickened by potatoes. If it all becomes absorbed by potatoes, add more. Season with thyme, salt and pepper. Cool slightly. Stir some of warm mixture into yogurt. Slowly add yogurt to chowder, stirring. Float a pat of butter on each serving. Makes 4 to 6 servings.

FRUIT SENEGALESE SOUP

A scrumptious use of leftover chicken and odds and ends of produce before marketing day! Rich and thick, this is an unusual main-dish soup.

1 large onion
1 stalk celery, with leaves
1 large apple, peeled
1 small sweet potato (1 cup diced)
1 large banana
1/4 cup butter

2 tbs. flour
2 tsp. curry powder, or to taste
2 cups chicken broth
1/2 cup dry white wine or vermouth
1 to 1-1/2 cups diced chicken meat
toasted coconut

Chop onion, celery and apple. Dice sweet potato. Slice banana. Melt butter in heavy 3-quart saucepan. Add onion, celery, apple and potato. Saute until tender, not browned. Add banana. Saute briefly. Add flour and curry. Cook over low heat, stirring, 3 to 4 minutes. Do not brown. Slowly pour in chicken broth, stirring constantly, cooking until smooth and slightly thickened. Cool. Puree mixture in blender. Add yogurt and wine. Season to taste. Chill well. Before serving, fold in diced chicken. Top with toasted coconut. Makes 6 to 8 servings.

SCANDINAVIAN FRUIT SOUP

For a special, hearty children's breakfast on a cold rainy day, spoon warmed fruit soup over oatmeal, splash with cream and top with yogurt.

1 pkg. (8 ozs.) dried apricots
1 pkg. (8 ozs.) dried peaches
1 pkg. (8 ozs.) dried pears
1 pkg. (8 ozs.) pitted prunes
1/2 cup raisins
2 qts. water
2 apples, peeled and cored
1/2 cup honey

2 tbs. lemon juice
1 3-inch thin slice lemon peel
2 3-inch cinnamon sticks
1/2 tsp. freshly-ground nutmeg
1/2 tsp. ground cloves
3 tbs. cornstarch
1 cup pineapple juice
1-1/2 cups yogurt

Soak dried fruits overnight in water. In the morning add apple, honey, lemon juice, peel and spices. Bring to boil. Reduce heat. Simmer until fruit is soft, about 1 hour. Remove lemon peel and cinnamon. Mix pineapple juice into cornstarch. Add to fruit mixture, stirring until slightly thickened. Cool. Stir in yogurt. Serve warm or cold, topped with yogurt. Makes 8 to 10 servings.

PLUM-RUM SOUP

Canned plums are transformed by a hint of spice and a dash of rum into a delightful dessert soup!

1 can (1 lb. 14 ozs.) purple plums in heavy syrup
1/2 cup firmly-packed brown sugar
2 tbs. cornstarch
1/2 tsp. cinnamon
1/4 tsp. salt
1 tbs. Myers' Jamaican rum
1 cup yogurt

Drain plums. Reserve 1-1/2 cups syrup. Remove pits from plums. Puree fruit in blender. Combine sugar, cornstarch, cinnamon and salt in saucepan. Add plum syrup, stirring to blend. Cook over medium heat, stirring, until slightly thickened. Add plums. Stir a small amount of warm plums into yogurt. Slowly add yogurt to plum mixture in pan. Heat gently to warm. Stir in rum. Spoon into sherbet glasses, top with yogurt. Makes 4 to 6 servings.

STRAWBERRY SOUP

Easy to make and tastes heavenly! Bacchus, himself, would cheer!

2 pkgs. (10 ozs. ea.) frozen sliced strawberries
2 tbs. arrowroot or cornstarch
1 cup orange juice
1/2 tsp. ground cinnamon
1 to 1-1/2 cups yogurt
1/2 cup port

Defrost strawberries. In saucepan bring strawberries to boil. Reduce heat. Simmer gently 4 to 5 minutes. Mix arrowroot with 1/4 cup orange juice. Slowly add to fruit. Stir in remaining orange juice and cinnamon. Simmer until thickened. Cool. Puree in blender. Add yogurt and port. Chill thoroughly. Garnish with yogurt flavored lightly with orange liqueur. Makes 4 to 6 servings.

VARIATION — In place of frozen strawberries, use 3 cups sliced fresh strawberries, 3/4 cup sugar and 1/2 cup water. Simmer 8 to 10 minutes.

62

TROPICAL BANANA SOUP

2 cups mashed bananas
2 cups yogurt
2 tbs. brown sugar
2 tbs. dark rum
1/2 tsp. cinnamon
diced banana
diced orange segments
toasted coconut

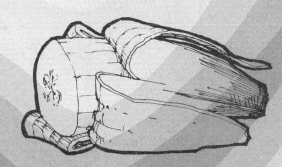

Place bananas, yogurt, brown sugar, rum and cinnamon in blender container. Cover. Blend on low speed until smooth. Chill 1 to 2 hours. Before serving, fold in diced banana and orange. Top each serving with yogurt and toasted coconut. Makes 4 to 6 servings.

SALADS AND VEGETABLES

Salad is the perfect poetic merging of Nature's gifts of greenery with the chef's inspired creativity! What could be more sublime than crunchy, leafy greens highlighted by a refreshing, tangy dressing? Whether crispy lettuce in its many varieties is served alone or imaginatively garnished with added munchables and savories, the green salad has become a daily menu favorite. Yogurt is at its zenith when used as a base for salad dressings. It combines artfully with all spices, herbs and flavorings to complement the many types of salad we enjoy. Yogurt is the best low-calorie substitute in salad dressings for sour cream, mayonnaise and oil—1 cup yogurt = 90 to 150 calories, 1 cup sour cream = 485 calories, 1 cup mayonnaise = 1587 calories, and 1 cup oil = a giant 2000 calories! Replace the traditional oil and vinegar blend with a zesty, slimming yogurt dressing. If you use packaged dry salad dressing mixes, such as green goddess, bleu cheese or French, substitute yogurt for all or part of the oil for a creamy low calorie variation, or mix one part yogurt to one part bottled dressing for a new flavor treat and a reduction in calories. Chill yogurt dressings at least 1 to 2 hours before serving, so the yogurt can re-thicken and flavors can fully blend. For a quick fruit salad combine 1 pound seedless grapes, 2/3 cup yogurt, 3 tablespoons brown sugar, 3 to 4 tablespoons grated Swiss or cheddar cheese and a dash of cinnamon.

Yogurt alone, or seasoned lightly with chopped mint, fresh dill, grated orange or lemon zest, or Parmesan cheese, is a savory topping to spoon over hot, steamed fresh vegetables. If you are fortunate enough to grow your own vegetables, enjoy the first flavor burst of an early Spring harvest, laced with a gently-flavored yogurt topping!

AMBROSIA

Items from the pantry shelf can be combined quickly to create this "ambrosial" treat. A marvelous buffet side dish, good with everything!

1 can (13 ozs.) pineapple tidbits
1 can (11 ozs.) mandarin oranges
1/4 cup halved maraschino cherries
1/2 cup chopped pecans
1 cup miniature marshmallows
1 cup shredded coconut
1/2 cup yogurt

Drain pineapple, oranges and cherries thoroughly. After draining, pat fruit with paper towels to remove any excess juice. Halve orange slices. Combine oranges, pineapple, pecans, marshmallows, coconut and yogurt. Chill 2 hours. Fold in cherries before serving. Makes 6 to 8 servings.

CARROT-PINEAPPLE MOLDED SALAD

This traditional favorite undergoes a dramatic change when blended with yogurt and molded into a fancy shape.

1 pkg. (3 ozs.) orange gelatin
1/2 cup boiling water
1 pkg. (3 ozs.) cream cheese, softened
1 can (8-1/4 ozs.) crushed pineapple
1-1/2 cups shredded carrots
1/2 cup raisins
1-1/4 cups yogurt
1 tbs. chopped fresh mint

Combine gelatin and boiling water in small saucepan. Stir until dissolved. Add cream cheese. Heat gently over very low heat, stirring, until cream cheese has completely blended into the liquid. Cool. Fold in remaining ingredients. Spoon into 4-cup mold. Chill several hours until set. Makes 6 to 8 servings.

WALDORF-CHEESE SALAD

The dressing recipe makes more than needed for this salad. Save the rest. It's delicious on chicken salad, or sliced bananas for breakfast!

Date-Cinnamon Dressing
2 cups diced unpeeled red apples
1/2 cup thinly-sliced celery
1/2 cup cubed cheddar cheese
1/3 cup chopped walnuts

Prepare dressing as directed and refrigerate. To make salad, combine apples, celery, cheese and walnuts with Date-Cinnamon Dressing. Makes 4 to 6 servings.

DATE-CINNAMON DRESSING — Combine 1 cup yogurt, 2 tablespoons honey, 1/3 cup pitted, chopped dates and 1/2 teaspoon cinnamon in blender container. Blend at medium speed 5 to 10 seconds. Do not puree dates completely. There should be recognizable date chips in the dressing. Chill 1 to 2 hours.

BEAN SPROUT SALAD

1 lb. bean sprouts
1/2 cup sliced green onion tops
1/4 lb. fresh mushrooms
1 cup yogurt
3 tbs. soy sauce
1 tbs. rice vinegar
1 tbs. sherry
2 tsp. sugar
2 tsp. toasted sesame oil*
1/4 tsp. grated fresh ginger
alfalfa sprouts
tomatoes
avocados

   Blanch bean sprouts one minute in pot of boiling water. Drain in colander. Rinse with cold water until sprouts are cold. *Drain well.* Chill. Thinly slice onions, measure, reserve 2 tablespoons. Clean and slice mushrooms. Combine

70

yogurt, soy, vinegar, sugar, sesame oil and ginger. Mix lightly with chilled sprouts, mushrooms and green onions. Serve on a bed of alfalfa sprouts on chilled salad plates. Surround with tomato wedges and avocado slices. Sprinkle with reserved green onion. Makes 4 servings.

VARIATION — Add 1 cup shredded chicken or pork or diced shrimp.

*Some supermarkets carry this, or it can be found in a Chinese grocery store.

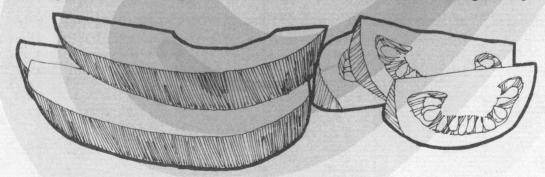

GUACAMOLE SALAD

Yogurt retards the darkening of avocados. To store guacamole for several hours, coat top of mixture with a thin layer of yogurt and mix in before serving.

8 medium-sized, ripe tomatoes
2 small green onions with tops
2 large avocados
1 to 2 tbs. fresh lime juice

1/2 to 3/4 cup yogurt
1 tsp. dried oregano leaves
1/2 tsp. salt
dash cayenne

Peel, seed and chop 2 tomatoes. To prepare onions, mince whites (2 table-spoons), thinly slice green tops (3 to 4 tablespoons). Mash avocados with lime juice. Combine avocados, chopped tomatoes, onions, yogurt, oregano, salt and cayenne. Chill 1 hour. Peel remaining tomatoes. Hollow out tomatoes with large spoon, leaving outside shell intact. Drain upside down on paper towels while avocado mixture chills. Fill tomatoes with avocado. Place on romaine lettuce leaves on chilled salad plates. Top with yogurt. Surround with tortilla chips for dipping. Makes 6 servings.

CHICKEN SALAD

Coconut-Pineapple Dressing, page 77
1 whole chicken (3 to 3-1/2 lbs.)
1 carrot
1 celery stalk
1 onion, quartered
sprig parsley

1 cup thinly-sliced celery
1 can (13 ozs.) pineapple tidbits
1/2 cup toasted almond slivers
1/2 cup sliced green onions with tops
1/2 cup sliced water chestnuts

    Remove giblets from chicken. Place whole chicken in large pot with carrot, celery, onion and parsley. Add water to just cover chicken. Cover pot. Bring to boil. Reduce heat, simmer 10 to 15 minutes. Remove pot from heat and cool chicken in liquid 1 hour. Skin and bone chicken. Dice meat. Combine chicken, celery, pineapple, almonds, green onions and water chestnuts. Lightly toss with Coconut-Pineapple Dressing. Garnish with additional toasted almonds. Makes 6 to 8 servings.
VARIATION — Substitute lichee fruit and macademia nuts for pineapple and almonds.

74

SALMON MOUSSE

Leftover salmon becomes a savory summer salad or an elegant addition to an hors d'oeuvre buffet table. Try making this with finely-shredded chicken.

2 cups flaked cooked salmon
1-1/2 cups yogurt
1/2 cup mayonnaise
1/2 cup *finely*-minced celery
1/4 cup *finely*-minced cucumber
2 tbs. *finely*-minced shallots
2 tbs. *finely*-minced parsley

4 tsp. fresh lemon juice
3/4 tsp. salt
1/2 tsp. prepared horseradish
1/2 tsp. dried dill weed, crushed
2 tbs. unflavored gelatin
1/2 cup dry vermouth
Whipped Lemon Dressing, page 77

Combine salmon with yogurt and mayonnaise, flaking finer with fork while mixing. Add celery, cucumber, shallots, parsley, lemon juice, salt, horseradish and dill. Mix well. Sprinkle gelatin over vermouth to soften. Heat gently until dissolved. Stir into salmon mixture. Pour into oiled 1-quart fish-shaped mold. Chill until set. Unmold on platter of romaine lettuce leaves. Serve with Whipped Lemon Dressing. Makes 6 to 8 servings.

CREAMY YOGURT DRESSING

This savory adaptation of the classic, oil-based dressing has many fewer calories than the original. Delicious with crispy lettuce salads!

3/4 cup yogurt
1/4 cup mayonnaise
1 small garlic clove, *finely* minced
2 tsp. Dijon-style mustard

1 tbs. lemon juice
1/4 to 1/2 tsp. freshly-ground pepper
1/2 tsp. salt
1 tbs. sugar

Combine all ingredients thoroughly. Chill several hours.

VARIATIONS — Add 1/4 cup crumbled bleu cheese *or* 1 tablespoon fresh or 1 teaspoon dried oregano, tarragon, basil *or* 1/4 cup chopped green onion *or* 1/3 cup crumbled bacon *or* 1 tablespoon tomato paste *or* chopped anchovy fillets *or* 1 to 2 chopped, hard-cooked eggs.

COCONUT-PINEAPPLE DRESSING

Good with chicken, fruit or seafood salads. Try 1/4 cup toasted almonds, ground, instead of coconut.

1/4 cup flaked coconut	3 tbs. pineapple juice
3/4 cup yogurt	1 tbs. orange marmalade
3 tbs. mayonnaise	1 tsp. dried tarragon

Toast coconut. Cool. Combine ingredients. Chill well.

WHIPPED LEMON DRESSING

1/3 cup yogurt	1/2 tsp. prepared mustard
1 tbs. fresh lemon juice	1/2 cup heavy cream, whipped

Combine yogurt, lemon juice and mustard. Fold in whipped cream. Chill.

HONEY AVOCADO CREAM

Serve with cold sliced turkey or cold cooked shrimp. Excellent with citrus fruit salad garnished with banana chips.

1 cup yogurt	3 tbs. fresh lime juice	1/4 tsp. dried mint leaves
1 ripe avocado	2 tbs. honey	1/4 tsp. salt

Puree in blender. Chill several hours.

SCANDINAVIAN DILL SAUCE

Serve with cold roast beef, chilled shrimp or barbecued lamb kebobs.

1/2 cup yogurt	2 tbs. honey	1 tbs. dried dill weed
1 tbs. prepared mustard	1 tbs. fresh lemon juice	

Combine ingredients. Chill several hours.

LOUIE DRESSING

1/2 cup yogurt
1 tbs. lime juice
1 tbs. minced shallot
2 tbs. bottled chili sauce
1/4 tsp. garlic powder
1/2 cup heavy cream, whipped

Combine yogurt, lime juice, shallot, chili sauce, garlic powder. Fold in whipped cream.

CAVIAR DIPPING SAUCE

1/2 cup mayonnaise
1/2 cup yogurt
1 tsp. Dijon-style mustard
1 tbs. lemon juice
1/4 tsp. freshly-ground pepper
1/8 tsp. garlic powder
1/4 cup heavy cream, whipped
2 ozs. caviar

Combine mayonnaise, yogurt, mustard, lemon juice, pepper and garlic powder. Chill 2 hours. Fold in whipped cream. Just before serving gently fold in caviar. Delicious with artichokes and shrimp.

APPLE PARSNIPS

Spice and apple juice highlight the hidden sweet nature of this vegetable. When parsnips are pureed, the tough core needn't be removed.

8 large parsnips
1 cup apple juice
1 cup yogurt
6 to 8 tbs. melted butter
1/3 cup firmly-packed brown sugar
1 tsp. salt

1/4 tsp. freshly-grated nutmeg
1 tbs. Calvados (optional)
brown sugar
nutmeg
soft butter

Peel and quarter parsnips. Cook with apple juice, covered, until tender. Puree in blender or food processor, in small batches if necessary. Add yogurt, butter, sugar, salt, nutmeg and brandy. Spoon parsnips into baking dish. Sprinkle with additional brown sugar and nutmeg, dot with butter. Bake in 350°F. oven 15 to 20 minutes. Makes 6 to 8 servings.

TOMATO-ZUCCHINI MEDLEY

1/2 lb. bacon
1 large onion, chopped
1/3 cup chopped green pepper
1 cup fresh or frozen corn kernels
2 zucchini, quartered lengthwise
4 firm, ripe tomatoes, halved

1/4 cup flour
seasoned salt
pepper
1-1/2 tsp. dried basil or oregano
1 cup yogurt
1/2 cup grated Parmesan cheese

In large skillet cook bacon until crisp. Remove from pan, drain. Crumble bacon, keep warm in oven. In bacon drippings saute onion and pepper until soft. Add corn. Cook 3 to 4 minutes longer. Remove vegetables from pan, draining with slotted spoon. Combine flour, salt and pepper. Lightly dust tomatoes and zucchini with flour mixture. Saute in remaining bacon drippings until tender. Place on warmed serving platter. Return onion mixture to pan. Add crumbled bacon and basil. Fold in yogurt. Heat until just warmed. Pour mixture over zucchini and tomatoes. Top with cheese. Place under hot broiler for a few seconds to melt cheese. Garnish with yogurt. Serve immediately. Makes 6 to 8 servings.

SPINACH SOUFFLE

Be sure to remove eggs and yogurt from refrigerator early to bring them up to room temperature before beginning this.

soft butter
4 tbs. grated Parmesan cheese
1 pkg. (10 ozs.) frozen chopped spinach
2 tbs. minced shallots
1/2 cup butter
1 tbs. fresh lemon juice
5 tbs. flour
1/2 cup hot milk

1 cup yogurt
1 tsp. salt
1/8 tsp. freshly-ground pepper
1/8 tsp. freshly-grated nutmeg
6 egg yolks
7 egg whites
scant 1/2 tsp. cream of tartar

Preheat oven to 400°F. Butter 8-cup souffle dish. Coat bottom and sides with 2 tablespoons cheese. Set aside. Defrost and drain spinach. Press out excess liquid. Saute shallots in 2 tablespoons butter. Add spinach and lemon juice. Cook over low heat, stirring often, until liquid has evaporated. Set aside. Melt remaining butter in top of double boiler set over direct heat. Add flour, salt, pepper and nutmeg. Cook, stirring, 2 to 3 minutes until bubbling, not brown. Remove from heat. Slowly add hot milk, whisking rapidly to smoothly blend. Cool slightly. Beat yolks into thickened mixture one at a time. Slowly add yolk mixture to yogurt. Pour mixture back into pan. Place over hot, not boiling, water. Cook, stirring, until thickened. Add warm spinach mixture. Whip egg whites with salt and cream of tartar until stiff, not dry. Stir 1/2 cup whites into spinach mixture. Gently fold in remainder of egg whites. Pour into prepared dish. Sprinkle with remaining cheese. Place in hot oven, immediately reduce heat to 375°F. Bake 40 to 45 minutes. Serve immediately. Makes 6 to 8 servings.

VARIATIONS — Serve with Mornay Sauce, page 95, but substitute chicken broth for clam broth in the recipe.

For a souffle with a "crown" — Before baking, take a knife or spatula and run a 1-1/2 inch deep groove around the souffle mixture about 1-1/4 inches from edge of dish.

EGGS, CHEESE AND SAUCES

Eggs and cheese combine with yogurt to create a wide variety of the most pleasing and delicate gastronomic treats. The egg works its magic in many ways. It is breakfast—scrambled, poached, omeletted. It is leavening in cakes, a thickener in sauces, a binder in casseroles. It is the egg which mystically builds lighter-than-air souffle castles. When teamed with yogurt, the egg sings in a harmonic blending as it scores new culinary symphonies. Yogurt brings a special lightness and savor to egg dishes. Stir in a few tablespoons of yogurt when mixing the eggs for your next omelette masterpiece. Add yogurt to eggs before scrambling, fold it into egg sauces, spoon it over baked eggs, or replace some of the milk with yogurt when making French toast.

Cheese becomes refreshingly delectable when wedded to yogurt. Yogurt complements and enriches cheese sauces, quiches, appetizers and desserts. Try a scoop of yogurt mixed with grated cheddar cheese and a hint of basil, spooned over sliced tomatoes for a snack or light lunch.

All three—yogurt, eggs and cheese—have a common fragility. High heat or prolonged cooking will destroy their delicacy. All should be at *room temperature* before combining with heated mixtures and cooked only over *low heat.*

85

EGGS FLORENTINE

Mornay Sauce, page 95*
1 lb. fresh spinach
3 tbs. butter
dash freshly-grated nutmeg
8 eggs
lemon juice or vinegar
1/2 cup grated Parmesan cheese

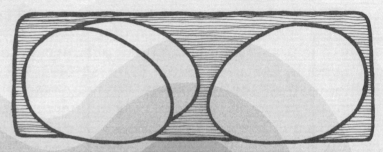

Prepare sauce. Set aside. Wash spinach and remove stems. Cook briefly in lightly-salted water. Drain well. Chop finely. Combine spinach, butter and nutmeg. Poach eggs in water containing lemon juice or vinegar (2-1/2 tablespoons per quart of water). Drain well. Spread spinach in four buttered ramekins or individual baking dishes. Place two poached eggs in each. Spoon sauce over eggs and spinach. Top with cheese. Brown under broiler 2 to 3 minutes. Makes 4 servings.

*Make Mornay Sauce using chicken broth instead of clam broth.

BACON 'N EGGS CASSEROLE

This must be chilled overnight before baking so that bread can absorb egg mixture. Instead of bacon, use sausage, smokies, ham, shrimp, pork or turkey.

1 lb. bacon
6 tbs. butter
10 slices egg bread
1/2 lb. fresh mushrooms, sliced
1-1/2 cups yogurt
1 cup milk

8 eggs
1 tsp. seasoned salt
1/2 tsp. freshly-ground pepper
1/2 tsp. dry mustard
1/2 cup sliced green onions
2 cups grated Swiss or cheddar cheese

Cook, drain and crumble bacon. Melt butter. Brush on bottom and sides of 13 by 9-inch baking dish. Trim off crusts and cube bread. Melt remaining butter in skillet. Saute mushrooms until tender. Using blender combine yogurt, milk, eggs, salt, pepper and mustard. In baking dish layer bread cubes, bacon, mushrooms, onions and 1 cup cheese. Pour egg mixture evenly over layers. Top with remaining cheese. Cover with foil. Chill overnight. Bake, covered in 325°F. oven 1-1/2 hours. Remove foil last 20 minutes to brown. Makes 6 to 8 servings.

SYLVIA'S WELSH RAREBIT

1/4 cup butter	1 lb. sharp cheddar cheese, grated
1/4 cup flour	1 cup yogurt
1 cup beer	English muffins
1/2 cup milk	1/2 cup chopped, salted peanuts
1 tsp. dry mustard	crisp bacon slices
1 tbs. Worcestershire sauce	tomato wedges

Melt butter in large saucepan. Add flour. Cook 2 to 3 minutes, until bubbling, not browned. Remove from heat. Add beer and milk, whisking to blend smoothly. Stir in mustard and Worcestershire. Return to heat. Cook gently until thickened. Slowly add cheese, stirring until melted. Cool slightly. Stir in yogurt. Spoon over split, toasted English muffins. Top with peanuts. Garnish with crisp bacon slices and tomato wedges. Makes 4 to 6 servings.

VARIATION — Stir in 1/2 cup chopped dill pickles, spoon over thick tomato slices. Garnish with bacon slices. Serve with Rye Krisp.

QUICHE LORRAINE

unbaked pie pastry
1/2 lb. diced bacon
1-1/2 cups chopped onion
1 cup yogurt
1 cup half and half
3 eggs

1/2 tsp. salt
1/4 tsp. freshly-ground pepper
1/4 tsp. freshly-grated nutmeg
2 tbs. chopped chives
1/4 cup grated Swiss cheese

Line 9-inch fluted quiche dish or deep-dish pie plate with pastry. Chill. Saute bacon until it begins to lightly color. Add onion. Continue to cook both until onion is tender and bacon is golden. Set aside. Using blender combine yogurt, cream, eggs, salt, pepper and nutmeg. Spread bacon and onions over bottom of pastry. Sprinkle with chives. Slowly and evenly pour yogurt mixture over filling. Top with cheese. Bake in 350°F. oven 35 to 45 minutes or until knife inserted in center of custard comes out clean. Cool on wire baker's rack 15 to 20 minutes until custard sets. Serve warm. Makes 6 to 8 servings.

MUSHROOM-SAUSAGE QUICHE

unbaked pie pastry
4 tbs. butter
1 onion, chopped
1 lb. fresh mushrooms, sliced
1 tbs. lemon juice
1/2 lb. bulk sausage
1 cup yogurt

1 cup half and half
3 eggs
1 tsp. salt
1/4 tsp. freshly-ground pepper
1/4 tsp. freshly-grated nutmeg
3 tbs. minced parsley

Line 9-inch fluted quiche dish or deep-dish pie plate with pastry. Chill. In butter, saute onion and mushrooms until tender. Add lemon juice. Continue to cook until liquid has evaporated. Remove from pan. Set aside. Saute sausage until brown and crumbly. Drain well. Using blender combine yogurt, half and half, eggs, salt, pepper and nutmeg. Place mushrooms and sausage in pastry. Slowly and evenly pour yogurt mixture over filling. Top with parsley. Bake in 350°F. oven 35 to 45 minutes or until knife inserted in center of custard comes out clean. Cool on wire baker's rack 20 to 25 minutes until custard sets. Serve warm. Makes 6 to 8 servings.

MIXED CHEESES QUICHE

Save bits and pieces of leftover cheese until there is enough for this.

unbaked pie pastry
1 cup yogurt
1 cup half and half
3 eggs
1 egg yolk
2 tbs. flour
1 tsp. prepared mustard

1 tsp. Worcestershire sauce
1/4 tsp. freshly-grated nutmeg
1/4 tsp. salt
freshly-ground pepper
2 cups *plus* 2 tbs. mixed grated cheese
2 to 4 tbs. crumbled bleu cheese
1/3 cup sliced green onion tops

Line 9-inch fluted quiche dish or deep-dish pie plate with pastry. Chill. Using blender combine yogurt, half and half, eggs, yolk, flour, mustard, Worcestershire, nutmeg, salt and pepper. Place cheese in crust, reserving 2 tablespoons. Add green onion tops. Slowly and evenly pour yogurt mixture over filling. Top with reserved cheese. Bake in 350°F. oven 35 to 40 minutes or until knife inserted in center of custard comes out clean. Cool on wire baker's rack 15 to 20 minutes until custard sets. Serve warm. Makes 6 to 8 servings.

CHEESE SOUFFLE

6 tbs. soft butter
2 tbs. grated Parmesan cheese
5 tbs. flour
1/2 cup hot milk
6 egg yolks
1 cup yogurt
1 cup shredded Gruyère cheese
2 ozs. crumbled bleu cheese
1 tsp. Dijon-style mustard
1 tsp. Worcestershire sauce
dash cayenne
7 egg whites
pinch salt
scant 1/2 tsp. cream of tartar

Butter 8-cup souffle dish with 2 tablespoons butter. Coat bottom and sides with Parmesan. Preheat oven to 400°F. Melt 1/4 cup butter in top of double boiler over direct heat. Add flour. Cook, stirring, 2 to 3 minutes. Remove from heat. Slowly add hot milk, whisking to blend. Cool slightly. Beat in yolks one at a time. Whisk mixture into yogurt. Return to heat over hot, not boiling, water. Add cheeses, stirring until melted. Mix in mustard, Worcestershire and cayenne. Whip egg whites with salt and cream of tartar until stiff, not dry. Stir 1/2 cup beaten whites into warm cheese mixture. Fold in remainder. Pour into souffle dish. Place in oven and reduce heat to 375°F. Bake 35 to 40 minutes, until puffed and golden brown. Serve immediately. Makes 6 to 8 servings.

SWEET NOODLE PUDDING (KUGEL)

1/2 cup chopped, dried apricots
1/2 cup golden raisins
1 cup boiling water
1 pkg. (7 ozs.) wide egg noodles
6 tbs. melted butter
1 cup yogurt
1 cup cottage cheese
3 eggs
1/2 cup sugar

1 tsp. cinnamon
1 tsp. vanilla
1/4 tsp. salt
1/2 cup drained, crushed pineapple
1/2 cup toasted, slivered almonds
1/2 cup crushed cornflakes
2 tbs. sugar
1/2 tsp. cinnamon

Soak apricots and raisins in boiling water for 1/2 hour. Drain. Cook noodles according to package directions. Drain well. Toss with 2 tablespoons butter. In separate bowl mix yogurt, cottage cheese, eggs, sugar, cinnamon, vanilla and salt. Combine noodles, apricots, raisins, yogurt mixture, pineapple and nuts. Pour into well-buttered 12 by 9-inch baking dish. Top with mixture of cornflakes, sugar and cinnamon. Drizzle with remaining butter. Bake in 350°F. oven 45 minutes. Cut into squares. Makes 8 to 10 servings. Serve with pot roast.

MORNAY SAUCE (for fish)

2 tbs. butter
2 tbs. flour
1 cup bottled clam juice
1 cup yogurt

3 egg yolks, lightly beaten
2/3 cup shredded Gruyere or Swiss cheese
1/8 tsp. dry mustard
salt and white pepper

Melt butter in top of double boiler over direct heat. Add flour. Cook until frothy, but not browned. Remove from heat. Slowly add clam juice, stirring to smoothly blend. Return to low heat. Cook, stirring, until thickened. In separate bowl combine yogurt and egg yolks. Add hot mixture by drops to yogurt mixture. Return sauce to top of double boiler. Place over hot, not boiling, water. Heat gently. Add cheese, stirring until melted. Season with mustard, salt and pepper.

VARIATION — To use Mornay Sauce with poultry or vegetables, substitute 1 cup rich chicken broth for the clam juice.

MOCK HOLLANDAISE SAUCE

Fewer calories than hollandaise sauce. Add sherry or herbs to vary.

2 tbs. butter   1 tsp. lemon juice
2 tbs. flour   1/4 tsp. salt
1 egg yolk   few grains cayenne
1 cup yogurt

Melt butter in top of double boiler. Add flour, cook 1 to 2 minutes, stirring. Remove from heat, cool slightly. Whisk in egg yolk. Return to heat. Slowly add yogurt. Continue heating and whisking until thickened. Do not overheat or let water boil. Add lemon juice, salt and cayenne. Use with fish, Eggs Benedict, vegetables.

VARIATION — Add 1/2 teaspoon grated orange zest. Spoon over steamed asparagus. Top with chopped cashews or grated Parmesan cheese.

MOUSSELINE SAUCE — Add 3 tablespoons heavy cream, whipped, and 3/4 teaspoon tarragon to Mock Hollandaise Sauce. Excellent with eggs, poached salmon or steamed vegetables.

TARTAR HOLLANDAISE — Fold into Mock Hollandaise 1/2 teaspoon Dijon-style mustard, 1 tablespoon *each* minced shallots, chopped, drained sweet pickle, chopped, drained green olives and pimientos, and minced parsley. Spoon over broiled fish.

BEARNAISE SAUCE — Combine 1 tablespoon fresh *or* 1 teaspoon dried tarragon, 1 tablespoon minced shallot, 1 tablespoon tarragon vinegar, 3 tablespoons dry white wine in small saucepan. Cook down until almost a glaze. Cool. Add to Mock Hollandaise Sauce in place of lemon juice. Flavor with added tarragon and chervil to taste. Serve with broiled meats.

CHORON SAUCE — Add 1 tablespoon tomato paste to Bearnaise Sauce. Serve with baked eggs, broiled meats and fish.

ENTREES

A good entree is essential to a successful meal. It is the focal point around which all other courses revolve. Yogurt breathes new life into old entree favorites.

Yogurt has been the mainstay of Indian curry dishes for centuries. It may also be used in place of milk, cream or sour cream in other familiar entrees such as beef stroganoff, Hungarian goulash, creamed eggs, chicken tetrazzini and shrimp newburg. Enrich casseroles and spaghetti sauce with yogurt. Yogurt lightens and moistens ground meat, meatloaf mixtures, tuna and salmon loaves. It makes a tenderizing marinade for meat and poultry. Marinate cubed turkey breast or lamb in a spicy yogurt blend before threading on skewers for grilling.

The tangy creaminess of a yogurt sauce complements the delicate flavor of seafood and poultry. Succulent chicken breasts, or broiled fresh fish, topped with a savory yogurt sauce makes a delicious entree low in both calories and cholesterol.

The entree ideas presented are designed to help you begin your own culinary odyssey into the world of yogurt. Invent and delight in your own unique yogurt specialties!

DAVE'S RAILROAD BEANS

These beans were created by my grandfather while working the railroads in the early 1900's. The pot of beans would gently bubble and simmer on the fire all day long as the train rumbled across the land. In the evening the wearied crew, lured to the caboose by the tantalizing aroma, would enjoy a hearty dinner.

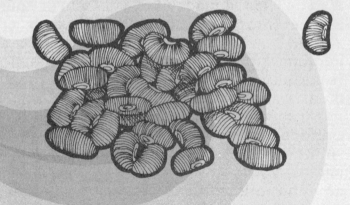

1 pkg. (1 lb.) dried red beans
3 large onions
3 large garlic cloves
2 lbs. ham
1/3 cup olive oil
2 cans (1 lb. 12 ozs. ea.) tomatoes
1 can (8 ozs.) tomato sauce
1 dried jalapeño pepper (optional)
1/2 lb. sharp cheddar cheese
1 cup yogurt

Cover beans with water, soak overnight. In the morning chop onions, mince

garlic. Cut ham into 1/2 to 3/4-inch dice. Saute onions and garlic in olive oil until translucent, but not browned, about 20 minutes. Add beans in their liquid, tomatoes, tomato sauce, ham and pepper. Cook over low heat 5 to 7 hours, stirring occasionally, until beans are tender. Remove pepper. Cool. Grate cheese. Add to beans slowly, stirring until melted. Add yogurt. Season to taste. Do not salt until end of cooking time—the ham and cheese often salt the beans sufficiently. Serve with cornbread. Makes about 3-1/2 quarts of beans.

Delicious as an entree, or use as an accompaniment to barbecued meats. The beans freeze well, and are even better when made a day or two ahead and the flavors have mellowed. If cooked ahead, omit cheese and yogurt. Just before serving, reheat and add cheese and yogurt.

101

CHICKEN LIVERS MADEIRA

A tasty entree for a luncheon or an after-theater supper! If served in a chafing dish, keep the flame low so sauce doesn't overheat.

6 tbs. butter
1 finely-chopped onion
1/2 lb. fresh mushrooms, sliced
1 lb. chicken livers
salt and pepper
1 tbs. flour

1/2 cup chicken broth
1/2 cup Madeira or sherry
1/2 tsp. dried thyme
2/3 cup yogurt
Almond Rice, page 103

Melt 4 tablespoons butter in skillet. Add onion and mushrooms. Saute until tender. Remove from pan with slotted spoon. Add remaining 2 tablespoons butter to pan with chicken livers. Sprinkle livers with salt and pepper, saute until no longer pink. Remove livers, keep warm. Stir flour into pan drippings. Cook over low heat for 1 to 2 minutes. Remove pan from heat. Slowly add broth and wine while stirring. Return to low heat. Cook until thickened. Add thyme and yogurt. Fold in livers and mushrooms. Serve over Almond Rice. Makes 4 servings.

ALMOND RICE

1 cup long-grained rice
1-1/2 cups chicken broth
1 cup water
1 cup green peas, fresh or frozen
1/3 cup toasted almond slivers
butter

Place rice, chicken broth and water in saucepan. Bring to boil. Reduce heat. Cover and simmer until rice is almost done, about 20 minutes. Add peas to rice. Don't stir in. Cover and simmer about 5 minutes more. Mix rice and peas with toasted almonds. Add butter to taste.

HONEY BAKED CHICKEN

While the chicken bakes, the marinade is transformed into a rich sauce to spoon over baked potatoes or rice.

1 whole chicken (3-1/2 to 4 lbs.), cut up
or chicken pieces of your choice
2 tbs. butter
4 tbs. flour
1/2 cup honey
1/4 cup prepared mustard (yes, 1/4 cup!)
1 tsp. salt
1 tsp. cinnamon or curry powder
1 cup yogurt
1/3 cup white wine

Wash chicken pieces and pat dry with paper towels. Melt butter in saucepan. Add flour, cook until bubbling. Stir in honey, mustard, salt and cinnamon. Remove from heat. Slowly add hot mixture to yogurt. Coat chicken pieces with sauce. Marinate 2 to 3 hours. Place in baking dish. Spoon on extra marinade. Pour wine in around edge of dish. Bake in 350°F. oven 1 hour or until chicken is done and coating browned. Skim off excess fat. Stir sauce to blend. Serve immediately.

PEACHY CHICKEN — Before baking, arrange 2 cups well drained, sliced canned peaches in baking dish. Lay coated chicken pieces on top. Cover with marinade. Bake. Try with apricots, pineapple or cherries.

PEANUT-APPLE CHICKEN — Add 1/2 cup chunky peanut butter or 3/4 cup chopped peanuts to yogurt marinade. Before baking, place 2 to 3 cups sliced cooking apples in baking dish. Lay coated chicken pieces on top. Cover with marinade. Bake.

SUPREMES WITH ORANGE-APPLE SAUCE

6 chicken breasts (12 halves)
salt and pepper
1/4 cup butter
1 tbs. grated orange zest
1 cup orange juice
1 cup peeled, finely-chopped apple

1/4 cup Calvados or brandy
2 tbs. *each* butter and flour
1/2 cup whipping cream
1 cup yogurt
orange sections
unpeeled apple slices

Split, bone and skin chicken breasts. Lightly salt and pepper. Saute briefly in butter until opaque. Add orange zest, juice and apple. Simmer, covered, 5 to 6 minutes. (Chicken breasts are very delicate. Do not overcook or they will become tough.) Remove chicken, keep it warm. Reduce remaining liquid to a glaze. Deglaze pan with brandy. Melt butter in pan. Add flour. Cook carefully 2 minutes. Remove from heat. Pour in cream, stirring. Add yogurt. Heat sauce gently, stirring, until thickened. Do not boil. Add chicken, basting with sauce until coated and heated through. Place chicken and sauce in heated chafing dish. Garnish with orange sections and apple slices. Serve with Rosa Marina Parmesan. Makes 12 small servings.

106

ROSA MARINA PARMESAN

Rosa marina is a rice-shaped pasta, a pleasant taste change from the usual rice accompaniment.

1 box (8 ozs.) rosa marina
1/3 cup butter
2 garlic cloves, crushed
1/2 cup grated Parmesan cheese
1 tsp. dried basil
salt and pepper

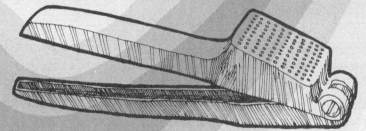

Cook rosa marina in boiling salted water 8 to 15 minutes until *al dente.* Check frequently. Drain. While pasta is cooking, melt butter in saucepan. Add garlic and cook over low heat 5 minutes. Remove garlic. To well-drained pasta, add butter, cheese and basil. Toss lightly. Season with salt and pepper. (Also delicious with broiled Italian sausages!)

SUPREMES AU CHAMPIGNONS

1/2 lb. fresh mushrooms
3 split chicken breasts, boned and skinned
6 tbs. butter
1 minced garlic clove
1 tbs. flour

1 tbs. lemon juice
1/4 cup white wine
1/2 tsp. tarragon
3/4 cup yogurt
salt and freshly-ground pepper

Clean and slice mushrooms. Poach chicken breasts or saute in 3 tablespoons butter until opaque. Remove from pan, keep warm. Add remaining butter to pan with garlic. Saute mushrooms in melted butter 4 to 5 minutes until most of liquid has evaporated. Sprinkle flour over mushrooms. Cook one minute. Stir in lemon juice, wine and tarragon. Remove from heat. Combine with yogurt. Return to low heat. Cook until thickened. Season with salt and pepper. Spoon over chicken. Makes 6 small servings.

SICILIAN BAKED SEA BASS

1 large onion
2 garlic cloves
2 tbs. olive oil
5 anchovy fillets, chopped
1 can (14 ozs.) Italian plum tomatoes
1/4 tsp. dried rosemary
or 1 tsp. fresh rosemary

1 tbs. minced parsley
1 tbs. whole capers
1/2 cup sliced green olives with pimientos
1 cup yogurt
freshly-ground pepper
4 sea bass fillets

Chop onions and mince garlic. Saute in olive oil with anchovies until onions are tender. Add tomatoes and liquid, rosemary and parsley. Simmer, stirring, until liquid is reduced to a very thick sauce. Fold in capers and olives. Cool slightly. Add to yogurt. Season with pepper. Place bass in buttered baking dish. Top with sauce. Bake in 350°F. oven 20 minutes or until fish flakes easily when tested with fork. Serve immediately. Makes 4 servings.

SOLE MORNAY WITH PEARS

Mornay Sauce, page 95
6 sole fillets (2 lbs.)
butter
poached fresh pears or sliced canned pears

Prepare sauce and keep warm until needed. Saute sole gently and quickly in melted butter. It is very delicate and needs to cook only 3 to 5 minutes. Place fish in buttered baking dish or in individual ramekins. Arrange pears on top of fish fillets. Liberally spoon Mornay Sauce over pears and fish. Place under broiler 2 to 3 minutes until sauce is bubbling and lightly browned. Garnish with parsley or fresh mint. Serve immediately. Makes 6 servings.

FILLET OF SOLE AU VELOUTE

Sole is garnished with a low-calorie veloute sauce. To vary the sauce, add sherry, 1/2 teaspoon dill or your favorite herb, grated lemon zest, or 1 teaspoon tomato paste mixed with 1/2 teaspoon basil.

2 tbs. finely-minced shallots
4 large sole fillets
1 cup white wine

VELOUTE SAUCE

2 tbs. butter
2 tbs. flour
1/2 cup fish stock *or* clam juice
1/2 cup yogurt
salt and pepper

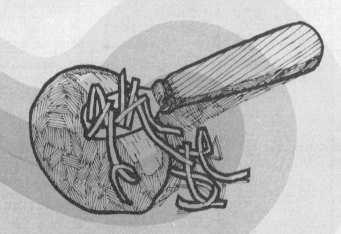

Sprinkle shallots on bottom of buttered shallow pan. Lay sole on top. Add wine. Cover. Poach gently 10 to 15 minutes or until fish flakes easily. Remove fish, keep warm. Strain liquid. Reserve 1/2 cup for sauce. Melt butter in top of double boiler over direct heat. Add flour. Cook 1 to 2 minutes until bubbling. Remove from heat. Add fish stock, stirring to blend. Place over hot, not boiling, water. Cook briefly until very thick. Add by drops to yogurt, stirring constantly. Return to pan. Add desired seasonings. Heat gently. Spoon over fish. Makes 4 servings.

CREAM VELOUTE SAUCE — Use 3 tablespoons *each* butter and flour and 1 cup fish stock. Mix 1/2 cup heavy cream with 1/2 cup yogurt before combining with hot ingredients. Heat until thickened. Season to taste. Makes enough sauce for 6 sole fillets.

BIFF A LA LINDSTROM

In Sweden these meat patties are often served on toast and topped with a fried egg—an interesting brunch idea accompanied by tomatoes and melon.

1/4 cup finely-chopped pickled beets
2 tbs. capers
1 tbs. finely-chopped dill pickle
4 tbs. minced onion
1 tbs. minced parsley
1 lb. extra lean ground beef
1/2 cup wheat germ
1 tsp. salt
freshly-ground pepper
1/2 cup yogurt
1 egg, plus 1 yolk
butter

An hour or two before using, chop beets, capers and pickles. Mince onion and parsley. Combine all with meat, wheat germ, salt and pepper. In separate bowl mix yogurt and eggs. Add to meat, mixing lightly. Set aside 1 to 2 hours. Shape into patties. Saute in sizzling butter. Serve with mashed potatoes topped with pan juices or in whole wheat rolls. Makes 4 servings.

VARIATION — Form into small meatballs. Saute in butter. Fill pita bread with meatballs, chopped tomatoes, alfalfa sprouts and yogurt.

STEAK au POIVRE

1 tbs. finely-crushed, black peppercorns*
butter
1-1/2 to 2 lbs. top sirloin steak
1 tbs. minced shallots
1 to 2 tbs. Cognac
1/2 cup heavy cream
1 tsp. Dijon-style mustard
1/2 cup yogurt
salt

   Set crushed peppercorns aside. Melt butter in heavy skillet. Saute steak until almost done, it will cook a bit more while sitting. Remove to heated serving platter. Keep warm. Add shallots to pan juices. Saute 1 to 2 minutes. Deglaze pan with Cognac. Add peppercorns, saute lightly. Pour in cream, stirring over low heat until thickened. Mix mustard with yogurt. Fold yogurt into pepper sauce. Salt to taste. Spoon over steak. Serve immediately. Makes 4 servings.
*Crush peppercorns with bottom of a heavy pot.

SPICY PLUM PORK CHOPS

8 center-cut pork chops
salt and pepper
2 tbs. butter or oil
1 can (1 lb.) purple plums
1/2 tsp. cinnamon or nutmeg
2 tbs. brown sugar
1 tbs. *each* catsup and lemon juice
1 cup yogurt
1/2 cup toasted pine nuts

Trim pork chops. Sprinkle lightly with salt and pepper. Brown in butter on both sides, about 5 minutes per side. Remove pits from plums. Add plums with their juice to meat. Cover. Cook in 350°F. oven about 25 minutes. Remove cover last 10 minutes. Remove meat from pan, keep warm. To pan juices and fruit, add cinnamon, sugar, catsup and lemon juice. Cook on top of stove, stirring, until blended. Combine with yogurt. Add pork chops, coat with sauce. Sprinkle with nuts. Serve immediately. Makes 8 small servings.

LAMB KORMA

Korma is a rich, spicy Muslim dish from Madras, India. Lamb is marinated in a yogurt sauce for several hours to absorb the full impact of the many flavors.

2 lbs. lamb sirloin*
1 cup yogurt
1 tsp. ground coriander
1 tsp. ground cumin
1/2 tsp. ground cinnamon
1/2 tsp. ground cardamom
1/2 tsp. chili powder
1/4 tsp. ground cloves
1 tsp. grated fresh ginger

2 large onions
2 large garlic cloves
3 large ripe tomatoes
4 tbs. olive oil
1 tsp. ground turmeric
1 cup water
salt
lemon juice
Cashew-Raisin Rice, page 119

Cut lamb into 1 to 1-1/2 inch cubes. Marinate several hours or overnight in yogurt, spices (except turmeric) and ginger. Chop onions and mince garlic. Peel, seed and chop tomatoes. In saucepan saute onions and garlic in olive oil until soft. Add tomatoes and turmeric. Cook carefully over low heat 2 minutes,

stirring. Do not burn. Add meat with yogurt-spice marinade and water. Cover. Simmer gently until meat is tender, 1-1/2 to 2 hours. Season with salt and lemon juice to taste. Serve over Cashew-Raisin Rice, topped with plain yogurt. Makes 6 servings.

CASHEW-RAISIN RICE — Cook rice according to package directions, *except* add an additional 1/4 cup water. For every cup of uncooked rice, add 1/2 cup of golden raisins along with rice to boiling water. When cooked, toss rice with 3 tablespoons butter and 1/2 cup toasted cashew pieces.

*Lamb shoulder or leg may be substituted for the sirloin.

BREADS

The wonderful, yeasty aroma of homemade bread baking in the oven summons a return of nostalgic, happy memories . . . a warm, cozy farmhouse kitchen . . . a handmade wooden table heaped with hot, crusty breads waiting to be spread with golden butter . . . giant stacks of steaming pancakes drizzled with thick, spicy honey . . . tantalizing fragrances reminiscent of joyful moments of childhood.

Home baking continues today as a creative art, a fulfilling pleasure and a reliable source of deliciously healthful food. Baked goods made with yogurt are delectably moist and tender, and their nutritive value is often increased.

You may substitute yogurt for all or part of the milk or water in yeast bread recipes. Gently warm the yogurt to the temperature required to activate the yeast. Be careful not to scald it. Add yogurt in place of buttermilk to recipes for rolls and biscuits. If the yogurt is thick, mix in a tablespoon or two of milk to thin it to the consistency of buttermilk. Substitute yogurt for sour cream or milk in coffeecake, waffle and doughnut batters. Remember to include 1/2 teaspoon of baking soda for each cup of yogurt used in the recipe. For richer flavor, add yogurt to packaged mixes for pancakes, cookies and cornbread.

SKILLET CORNBREAD

Cousin to the Southern spoon breads, this is a tender "fork" bread with a thin layer of creamy custard in the center.

3 tbs. butter
1-1/3 cups yellow cornmeal
1/3 cup sifted all-purpose flour
3 tbs. sugar
1 tsp. baking powder
1 tsp. baking soda
1 tsp. salt
1 cup yogurt
2 eggs, lightly beaten
2 cups milk
1/2 cup drained canned corn kernels

Melt butter in 9-inch heavy skillet in 400°F. oven while preparing batter. Sift together dry ingredients. In separate bowl beat together yogurt, eggs, and 1 cup milk. Add to dry ingredients with corn. Mix only until just moistened. Pour batter into hot skillet. Slowly pour remaining 1 cup milk evenly over top of batter. Do not stir in. During baking, milk will settle and form custard layer in middle of bread. Bake in 400°F. oven 35 minutes. Do not overbake! Cut into wedges. Serve immediately with butter and honey (and a fork!). Makes 6 to 8 servings.

VARIATION — Add grated cheese or crumbled bacon to batter before baking.

BLUEBERRY-PECAN TEA BREAD

2 cups sifted all-purpose flour
1 tsp. *each* baking powder and baking soda
1 tsp. cinnamon
1/2 tsp. salt
1/4 cup sugar
1/4 cup firmly-packed brown sugar

1 cup yogurt
1 egg
1/4 cup melted butter, cooled
1 tsp. grated lemon zest
1 cup fresh or frozen blueberries
1/2 cup chopped pecans

Sift together flour, baking powder, soda, cinnamon and salt. Stir in sugars. In separate bowl combine yogurt, egg, butter and lemon zest. Add to dry ingredients all at once, stirring until just moistened. Fold in berries and nuts. Spoon into greased 9 by 5-inch loaf pan. Bake in 350°F. oven 45 minutes or until done. Makes 1 loaf.

CARROT-COCONUT BREAD

Yogurt has replaced much of the usual oil in this carrot bread. Mellow bread in refrigerator a day or two before serving. Delicious toasted and buttered!

2 cups all-purpose flour
1-1/2 tsp. baking soda
1 tsp. baking powder
1/2 tsp. salt
2 tsp. cinnamon
3 eggs
1/2 cup sugar

1/2 cup firmly-packed brown sugar
1/4 cup oil
3/4 cup yogurt
1-1/2 cups shredded carrots
1-1/2 cups shredded sweetened coconut
1 cup chopped walnuts
1/2 cup raisins

Sift together flour, soda, baking powder, salt and cinnamon. Set aside. In large mixing bowl, beat eggs until fluffy. Blend in sugars, oil and yogurt. Stir in carrots, coconut, nuts and raisins. Add dry ingredients all at once, stirring just until well blended. Spoon into buttered 9 by 5-inch loaf pan. Bake in 350°F. oven 1 hour or until center tests done. Remove from pan, cool on wire rack. Wrap in foil. Chill. Bring to room temperature before serving.

MIXED GRAIN MUFFINS

4 tbs. butter
2 tbs. honey
1/2 cup cornmeal
1/2 cup whole wheat flour
1 tsp. *each* baking powder and baking soda
1/2 tsp. salt
1/4 cup wheat germ
3/4 cup yogurt
1 egg, beaten
1/3 cup chopped walnuts

Melt butter and honey together in small saucepan. Set aside. Sift together cornmeal, flour, baking powder, soda and salt. Stir in wheat germ. In separate bowl mix yogurt, egg, butter and honey. Add with nuts to dry ingredients. Combine quickly until just moistened. Fill buttered muffin cups 2/3 full. Bake in 350°F. oven 20 to 25 minutes. Makes 12 medium muffins.
VARIATION — Add grated cheese or crumbled bacon to batter before baking.

CRANBERRY-ORANGE MUFFINS

3/4 cup fresh or frozen cranberries
1-1/4 cups sugar
2 cups sifted all-purpose flour
1 tsp. *each* baking powder and baking soda
1/2 tsp. salt
1/2 tsp. freshly-grated nutmeg

1 egg, beaten
1 cup yogurt
1 tsp. grated orange zest
1/4 cup melted butter, cooled
1/2 cup chopped walnuts

Coarsely chop cranberries. Mix with 1/2 cup sugar. Set aside. Sift together flour, baking powder, soda, salt, nutmeg and remaining sugar. In separate bowl mix yogurt, egg, orange zest and melted butter. Add to dry ingredients all at once, stirring until just moistened. Fold in cranberries and nuts. Batter will be thick. Fill buttered muffin cups 2/3 full. Bake in 350°F. oven 20 to 25 minutes. Makes 24 medium muffins.

IRISH RAISIN BREAD

2-1/2 cups unsifted all-purpose flour
1-1/2 tsp. baking powder
1/2 tsp. baking soda
1/2 tsp. salt
3 tbs. sugar
1 cup raisins or currants
1-1/2 tsp. caraway seeds (optional)
2 egg yolks
3 tbs. melted butter
3/4 cup yogurt

Combine flour, baking powder, soda, salt and sugar. Sift over raisins. Add caraway. Beat egg yolks and butter into yogurt. Stir into dry ingredients until blended. Turn dough out on lightly-floured board. Knead until smooth, about 2 minutes. Shape dough into round loaf. Press into 8-inch round cake pan. With knife, cut cross on top of loaf. Bake in 375°F. oven about 40 minutes. Cool. Serve warm or cold, cut into wedges. Makes 8 servings.

HERBED CHEESE CASSEROLE BREAD

2-1/2 cups unsifted flour
2 tbs. sugar
1-1/2 tsp. salt
1 pkg. (1/4 oz.) dry yeast
1 cup yogurt

2 tbs. butter
1 cup grated cheddar cheese
1 egg yolk
2 tsp. dried dill, crushed

Combine 1 cup flour, sugar, salt and dry yeast in mixing bowl. Heat yogurt and butter in saucepan until warm, not hot. Slowly add to dry ingredients while mixing on low speed of electric mixer. Beat 2 minutes on medium speed. Add cheese, egg yolk, dill and 1/2 cup flour. Beat at high speed 2 minutes. Add enough more flour to make stiff batter. Beat until well blended. Cover. Let rise in warm place until doubled, about 45 minutes. Stir batter down. Place in greased 1-quart casserole. Bake in 375°F. oven 45 minutes or until done. Cool on wire rack. Cut into wedges. Serve warm with butter. Makes 8 servings.

PANETTONE

This Italian holiday bread, served traditionally at Christmas and Easter, becomes an elegant coffeecake for a special-occasion brunch.

2-1/2 to 3 cups sifted flour
1/3 cup sugar
1/2 tsp. salt
2 pkgs. (1/4 oz. ea.) dry yeast
1/2 cup yogurt
1/3 cup butter
3 egg yolks
1/4 cup chopped glacéd cherries
1/4 cup raisins
1/4 cup lightly-toasted pine nuts
1 tsp. anise seed
3/4 tsp. grated lemon zest

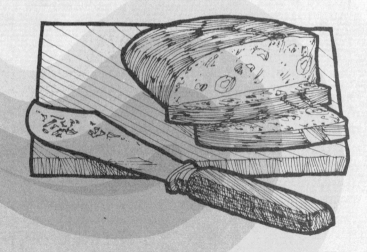

In mixing bowl combine 1 cup flour, sugar, salt and dry yeast. Heat yogurt and butter in small saucepan until butter is melted and yogurt is warmed. Slowly add to dry ingredients while beating at medium speed on electric mixer. Beat 2 minutes, scraping bowl. Add egg yolks and 1/2 cup flour. Beat at high speed 2 minutes. Stir in cherries, raisins, nuts, anise and lemon zest. Add enough additional flour to make a soft dough. Turn out onto lightly-floured board. Knead until smooth and elastic, 6 to 8 minutes. Place in oiled bowl, lightly oil top of dough. Cover. Let rise in warm place until doubled, about 1 hour. Punch dough down. Cover. Let rise again until almost doubled, about 1/2 hour. Shape into round loaf. Place on greased baking sheet. With knife, cut a cross on top of ball. Cover. Let rise again until doubled, about 1 hour. Brush top with melted butter. Bake in 350°F. oven 30 to 40 minutes. Brush with melted butter again. Cool on wire rack. Makes 1 loaf.

YOGURT PANCAKES

1/4 cup butter
2 tbs. honey
1-1/2 cups flour

1 tsp. baking soda
1/2 tsp. baking powder
1/2 tsp. salt

1/4 cup wheat germ
1-1/2 cups yogurt
2 eggs, separated

Melt butter and honey in small saucepan. Set aside. Sift together flour, soda, baking powder and salt. Stir in wheat germ. In separate bowl beat together yogurt, egg yolks, butter and honey. Add to dry ingredients, mixing just until moistened. Whip egg whites until stiff, but not dry. Fold into batter. Cook on medium-hot griddle. Serve with Honey Butter.

HONEY BUTTER — Cream together 1/2 cup soft butter, 3 tablespoons honey, 1/2 teaspoon cinnamon.

VARIATIONS — Add any of these to batter before folding in egg whites, nuts, corn, coconut, chocolate bits, blueberries, grated cheese, grated apple with cinnamon, crumbled bacon, chopped dates, grated orange or lemon zest, diced banana, spices, drained crushed pineapple, minced ham, raisins.

ORANGE-PECAN WAFFLES

1 cup whole wheat flour
1 cup all-purpose flour
3 tsp. baking powder
1 tsp. baking soda
1/2 tsp. salt
1/3 cup wheat germ
1/2 cup finely-chopped pecans

1-1/4 cups yogurt
3/4 cup orange juice
3 eggs, separated
1/2 cup melted butter
4 tbs. honey
2 tbs. grated orange zest
1/4 tsp. cream of tartar

Sift flours, baking powder, soda and salt. Stir in wheat germ and nuts. In separate bowl combine yogurt, juice, egg yolks, butter, honey and orange zest. Add to dry ingredients all at once, mixing to just moisten. Beat egg whites with cream of tartar until stiff, not dry. Fold into batter. Bake in oiled waffle maker. Top with melted butter, powdered sugar and chopped pecans or Pecan Butter.

PECAN BUTTER — Beat until fluffy, 1/2 cup soft butter, 1 cup brown sugar, 3 tablespoons yogurt, 1 teaspoon dark rum, 1/4 teaspoon cinnamon. Add 1/2 teaspoon orange zest and 1/2 cup finely-chopped pecans.

DESSERTS

We all love sweets. The great restaurants of the world pay tribute nightly to the splendid artistry of their dessert chefs. Sumptuously-laden carts roll forth with their beautiful displays—baskets bountifully filled with luscious fruits and berries, platters of magnificent cakes and tarts, silver buckets heaped high with creamy sorbets, and bowls of Eden-inspired sauces. The satiated appetite is tempted, revived and happily indulged once again! In our homes, whether at a cozy family dinner, a relaxed convivial evening with friends, or an elegant formal dining party, we serve dessert as the perfect finishing touch to an enjoyable meal.

The versatility of yogurt shines in the dessert course. A simple yogurt and fruit dessert is a refreshing conclusion to a heavy meal. Yogurt combines equally well with thick cream, jam and cake into an elegant English Trifle. Sweet, creamy, low calorie frozen yogurt is an ideal dessert. Cakes have a more delicate texture when made with yogurt and stay moist and fresh for several days. New adaptations of traditional fruit pies can be made with yogurt. Puddings, custards and mousses are all enhanced by the addition of yogurt.

For an easy, delicious dessert, slice fresh bananas, peaches, apricots, strawberries, figs or any other fruit in season into a large, glass serving bowl. Liberally spoon on yogurt or drained yogurt, top with honey or brown sugar and sprinkle with coconut, wheat germ or nuts. Try this layered into individual serving dishes for a nutritious, low calorie, light lunch. Mix honey and cinnamon into yogurt cheese and serve with sliced fresh pears or apples, or top hot fruit pie with sweetened yogurt cheese.

With ingenuity and a spirit of adventure, you can create marvelous new yogurt desserts from any of your favorite recipes!

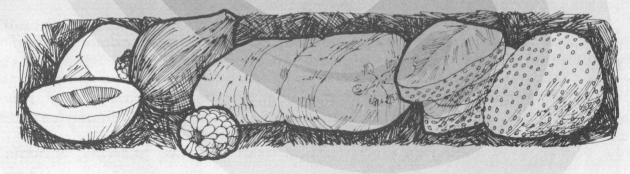

LIME MOUSSE WITH RASPBERRY-PLUM SAUCE

1 tbs. unflavored gelatin
4 tbs. lime juice
4 eggs, separated
3/4 cup sugar
2 tsp. grated lime zest

1 cup yogurt
pinch salt
scant 1/2 tsp. cream of tartar
5 tsp. green creme de menthe
Raspberry-Plum Sauce

Soften gelatin in lime juice. Beat egg yolks until creamy. Slowly add 1/2 cup sugar, beating until eggs are pale and thick. Fold in lime zest and gelatin. Cook in top of double boiler over hot, not boiling, water until thickened. Stir constantly. Cool. Fold in yogurt. Beat egg whites with salt and cream of tartar until soft peaks form. Add remaining 1/4 cup sugar, beating until stiff and glossy. Beat in liqueur. Fold into yogurt mixture. Spoon into individual parfait glasses. Chill until set. Serve with Raspberry-Plum Sauce. Makes 8 servings.
RASPBERRY-PLUM SAUCE — Drain 1 package (10 ozs.) frozen raspberries. Combine juice in saucepan with 1 tablespoon cornstarch, 2 tablespoons sugar, 3 tablespoons plum jam. Cook, stirring, until thickened. Fold in berries and 1 tablespoon Framboise or Kirsch. Cool.

PUMPKIN-PECAN PARFAIT

1 tbs. unflavored gelatin
1/2 cup orange juice
1-1/2 cups canned pumpkin
3/4 cup firmly-packed brown sugar
1 tsp. cinnamon
1/2 tsp. ground ginger
2 egg yolks
3/4 cup yogurt

1 cup chopped pecans
2 tsp. vanilla
1 tsp. grated orange zest
1 to 2 tbs. dark rum (optional)
3 egg whites
1/4 tsp. cream of tartar
1/2 cup sugar

Soften gelatin in orange juice. Combine in saucepan with pumpkin, sugar, spices and egg yolks. Cook over medium heat, stirring, until mixture *almost* comes to boiling point. Do not boil. Cool. Fold in yogurt, nuts, vanilla, orange zest and rum. Beat egg whites with cream of tartar until soft peaks form. Add sugar, beating until stiff and glossy. Fold into pumpkin mixture. Spoon into parfait glasses. Chill several hours until set. Garnish with yogurt and chopped pecans. Makes 6 to 8 servings.

EGGNOG GELATIN

For a festive holiday buffet, double this recipe and fold in squares of red and green gelatin before chilling. It will more than fill a 3-quart mold. Pour the extra into a small mold—a lovely take-home gift for a special friend!

3 tbs. unflavored gelatin
1/4 cup honey
1 qt. fresh dairy eggnog
1-1/2 cups yogurt
2 to 3 tbs. Myers' Jamaican rum
1/4 tsp. freshly-grated nutmeg

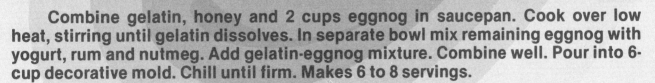

Combine gelatin, honey and 2 cups eggnog in saucepan. Cook over low heat, stirring until gelatin dissolves. In separate bowl mix remaining eggnog with yogurt, rum and nutmeg. Add gelatin-eggnog mixture. Combine well. Pour into 6-cup decorative mold. Chill until firm. Makes 6 to 8 servings.

STRAWBERRIES WITH BANANA CREAM

1 qt. fresh strawberries, sliced
sugar
2 to 3 tbs. Kirsch (optional)
3/4 cup yogurt
2 ripe bananas

3 tbs. honey
2 tbs. Grand Marnier or orange juice
1/2 cup heavy cream, whipped
Walnut Poundcake, page 150

Slice strawberries. Sugar lightly and marinate in Kirsch until serving time. Combine yogurt, bananas, honey and liqueur in blender. Fold in whipped cream. Chill. To serve spoon strawberries over Walnut Poundcake. Top with Banana Cream. Garnish with sliced strawberries and sprigs of fresh mint. Pass a bowl of honey to drizzle on top.

VARIATION — Layer strawberries and Banana Cream in stemmed dessert glasses.

ENGLISH TRIFLE

8 to 10 large coconut macaroons (2 cups crumbled)
5 to 6 tbs. Myers' Jamaican rum or sherry
2 pkgs. (3-3/4 ozs. ea.) Jello French vanilla pudding
1 cup *each* half and half and milk
2 tsp. vanilla
2 cups yogurt
1 loaf-type poundcake, sliced
1 pkg. spongecake ladyfingers
1-1/4 cups raspberry or apricot jam
1 cup heavy cream, whipped

Crumble macaroons, soak in 3 tablespoons rum. Combine pudding, cream and milk in top of double boiler. Cook, stirring, until very thick. Add vanilla. Cool 15 minutes. Fold into yogurt. Line bottom of 3-quart glass bowl with half of cake. Line sides of bowl with ladyfingers. Sprinkle rum on cake slices. Layer half of jam, macaroons, and pudding. Repeat layering, beginning with rum-sprinkled cake. Top with whipped cream. Chill several hours. Makes 12 servings.

PEACH CLAFOUTI

This puffs in the oven like a souffle, then falls to a creamy, fruit-filled custard. Try using fresh cherries and cinnamon or other fresh or canned fruits.

soft butter
2 tbs. powdered sugar
2 cups sliced fresh peaches
or 1 can (30 ozs.) sliced peaches, drained
1 cup half and half
1 cup yogurt

3 eggs
1/4 cup flour
pinch salt
4 tbs. sugar
1 tsp. vanilla
1/4 tsp. almond extract

Butter 9-inch round baking dish, sprinkle with powdered sugar. Arrange peaches in baking dish. Using blender mix half and half, yogurt, eggs, flour, salt, sugar, vanilla and almond extract. Pour carefully over fruit. Bake in 375°F. oven 45 to 55 minutes, or until puffed and golden. Cool. Dust with powdered sugar. Serve slightly warm with light cream yogurt, page 17.
VARIATION — Mix 1/2 teaspoon nutmeg with 1 can (1 lb. 5 ozs.) prepared fruit pie filling. Spoon into unbaked crust. Pour yogurt mixture over filling. Bake.

142

APRICOT-PISTACHIO RICE CREAM

2 cups milk
2 cups half and half
3/4 cup sugar
1/2 cup raw long-grained rice
1 3-inch cinnamon stick
1 cup shelled pistachio nuts
1 can (1 lb. 14 ozs.) whole apricots
1 cup yogurt
2 tbs. Amaretto liqueur
or 1/4 tsp. almond extract
2 egg whites
1/4 tsp. cream of tartar
3 tbs. sugar

Combine milk, half and half, sugar, rice and cinnamon in top of double boiler. Cook slowly over hot water until rice absorbs liquid. Stir occasionally. This may take as long as 2 hours. Cool. Blanch pistachios in boiling water 1

minute to remove skins. Drain apricots. Remove pits. Puree. Fold apricots into rice with yogurt and liqueur. Beat egg whites with cream of tartar until soft peaks form. Slowly add sugar, beating until stiff and glossy. Fold into rice with nuts. Spoon into large serving bowl. Chill. Makes 8 to 10 servings.

CREAMY RICE PUDDING — Cook rice, milk, half and half, sugar and cinnamon with 1/2 cup raisins added. Cool. Fold in 1 cup yogurt. Serve warm or cold.

DANISH APPLE PIE

unbaked pie pastry
1/4 cup sugar
1/4 cup firmly-packed brown sugar
2 tbs. cornstarch
1/4 tsp. salt
4 cups thinly-sliced, peeled cooking apples
few drops lemon juice
1 cup yogurt
1 egg
1/2 tsp. vanilla

Line 9-inch deep-dish pie pan with pastry. Chill. Preheat oven to 400°F. Combine sugars, cornstarch and salt. Mix with apples. Place in pastry. Sprinkle with lemon juice. Bake in preheated oven 20 to 25 minutes until apples are almost tender. Using blender combine yogurt, egg and vanilla. Reduce oven heat to 350°F. Pour yogurt mixture over apples. Bake 30 minutes more until custard is set and apples are done. Cool 15 minutes. Sprinkle on Topping. Cool half hour more before serving. Serve warm with yogurt. Makes 6 to 8 servings.

TOPPING

1/4 cup slivered almonds, toasted and finely-ground
1/2 cup firmly-packed brown sugar
1 tsp. cinnamon

Mix together and sprinkle on pie as directed.

VARIATION — Before adding yogurt mixture to pie, spread hot apples with 1/4 cup marmalade.

FUDGE BROWNIES

1/2 cup butter
3 ozs. unsweetened chocolate
2 eggs
1 cup sugar
1/3 cup yogurt
2 tsp. vanilla
3/4 cup all-purpose flour
1/4 tsp. baking soda
1/4 tsp. salt
1/2 cup chopped walnuts

Melt butter and chocolate in top of double boiler over hot water. Cool. Beat eggs until foamy. Slowly add sugar, beating until thick. Stir in chocolate, yogurt and vanilla. Sift flour, soda and salt together. By hand, fold dry ingredients into chocolate mixture until well blended. Stir in nuts. Spread into 9 by 13-inch buttered pan. Bake in 350°F. oven 20 to 25 minutes. Cool in pan. Cut into squares. Makes 24 brownies.

OATMEAL CAKE WITH BROILED COCONUT TOPPING

1 cup quick-cooking oatmeal
1 cup yogurt
1/2 cup water
1-1/2 cups sifted all-purpose flour
1 tsp. baking powder
1/2 tsp. baking soda

1/2 tsp. salt
1 tsp. cinnamon
1/2 cup soft butter
1 cup firmly-packed brown sugar
2 eggs
1 tsp. vanilla

Soak oatmeal in yogurt and water for 1/2 hour. Sift flour with baking powder, soda, salt and cinnamon. Set aside. Cream butter, sugar, eggs and vanilla. Add flour alternately with oatmeal, beginning and ending with flour. Pour into buttered 9 by 9-inch cake pan. Bake in 350°F. oven 45 to 50 minutes. Spread topping evenly on warm cake. Place cake under broiler 2 to 3 minutes until top is golden and bubbling. Cool. Cut into squares. Makes 8 to 10 servings.

BROILED COCONUT TOPPING — Combine 1/2 cup firmly-packed brown sugar, 1/4 cup melted butter, 1/4 cup half and half, 1-1/4 cups shredded coconut, 1/2 cup chopped nuts and 1/2 teaspoon cinnamon.

WALNUT POUNDCAKE

2-1/2 cups sifted all-purpose flour
1 tsp. baking powder
1 tsp. baking soda
1/2 tsp. salt
1 cup soft butter
2 cups sugar

3 eggs
2 tsp. vanilla
1 tsp. cinnamon or freshly-grated nutmeg
1-1/4 cups yogurt
3/4 cup chopped walnuts

Sift together dry ingredients. Set aside. Cream butter and sugar. Add eggs one at a time, beating well after each addition. Mix in vanilla and cinnamon. Add dry ingredients alternately with yogurt, beginning and ending with flour mixture. Fold in nuts. Bake in buttered and floured bundt pan in 350°F. oven 55 to 60 minutes or until foodpick inserted in cake comes out clean. Cool in pan 45 minutes. Invert on plate. Dust with powdered sugar. Or, while cake is warm, spoon on glaze.

BASIC GLAZE — Combine 1 cup sifted powdered sugar, 2 tablespoons juice or liqueur, and 2 tablespoons melted butter. Prick top of cake. Spoon on glaze.

150

CHOCOLATE-CHOCOLATE CHIP POUNDCAKE — Omit cinnamon. Add 6 ounces melted semi-sweet baking chocolate to batter before adding flour. Fold in 1 cup semi-sweet chocolate bits before baking. Spoon chocolate syrup on warm cake if desired.

RAISIN-SPICE POUNDCAKE — Change spice in recipe to 2 teaspoons instant coffee powder, 1 teaspoon cinnamon, and 1/2 teaspoon *each* ground cloves, ginger and grated nutmeg. Fold in 1/2 cup raisins with the nuts.

ORANGE-POPPYSEED POUNDCAKE — Omit spice if desired. Add to batter 1 tablespoon grated orange zest, 1/4 cup frozen orange concentrate (defrosted), and 4 tablespoons poppyseeds. Use orange liqueur in basic glaze.

COCONUT POUNDCAKE — Omit cinnamon. Fold 1 cup flaked coconut and 1/2 teaspoon almond or lemon extract before baking. Glaze with 1 cup sifted powdered sugar, 3 tablespoons melted butter and 1 tablespoon lemon juice.

FROZEN YOGURT

Frozen yogurt is the most popular food sensation to come along in years! It has captured the attention of everyone and is competing vigorously for the hearts of ice cream and frozen dessert lovers everywhere. Frozen yogurt is found scooped into cones, covered with nuts and crunchy toppings, nestled in crisp lettuce leaves, swirled into drinks, surrounded by juicy fresh fruits, and crowned by whipped cream. Specialty yogurt shops flourish. Supermarkets, ice cream manufacturers, and dairy companies all celebrate the American love affair with frozen yogurt. As people increasingly become more health conscious and aware of the necessity for good nutrition, they turn to more wholesome foods. Frozen yogurt appeals as both a healthful food and a sweet dessert. Joyfully, it often has only one-third to one-half the calories of the same amount of ice cream!

Homemade frozen yogurt is delicious and surpasses the quality of commercial products. It is tangy, rich and creamy, and can be made to contain fewer calories. The freshness and purity of the ingredients are never in question. Commercial varieties of frozen yogurt usually contain some combination of artificial flavoring and coloring and chemical preservatives. Homemade frozen yogurt is free from harmful additives and provides many important elements of sound

153

nutrition while it also satisfies that eternal yen for a sweet, refreshing dessert! It is easy to make at home and is far more economical than ready-made frozen yogurt . . . an oasis of welcome relief in today's costly world!

Flavor varieties and combinations are infinite! Luscious red strawberries from your garden, perfumy sun-ripened peaches from your orchard, marmalades and jams of summer canning projects, homemade applesauce, a seasonal rum-pot melange—all uniquely enhance the flavor of your own frozen yogurt. Pluck fresh mint from your herb garden to create a cooling finish to a dinner on a sultry summer evening. If you are not a grow-your-own enthusiast, hand-pick your favorite in-season fruits from the abundant selections at your market or health food store for equally inventive frozen yogurt desserts. Transform lemons or limes into a zesty palate refresher. Try a melon freeze or an avocado honey cream. Begin with the recipes here, then let your own imagination take flight! Unlimited tantalizing possibilities await your discovery!

MAKING FROZEN YOGURT — GENERAL INFORMATION

<u>YOGURT</u> — Homemade yogurt or commercial yogurt may be used in all frozen yogurt recipes. If you use commercial yogurt, be sure to choose one which is *fresh* with a tang you enjoy. The type of yogurt you select will depend upon your personal taste preference and the degree of your concern with butterfat and calorie content. Lowfat yogurt interchanges perfectly with whole milk yogurt and makes a frozen yogurt of equal quality. These recipes were all standardized with either a fresh dairy lowfat yogurt or a homemade lowfat yogurt with added dry milk powder (see page 16). For a frozen dessert with fewer calories, substitute nonfat milk yogurt. Nonfat frozen yogurt is slightly less creamy.

Flavor of your frozen yogurt will vary according to the tang of the particular yogurt you choose. If you use a highly tart yogurt and want to diminish the tang, increase the sweetener in the recipe to taste.

Commercial yogurts often contain extra thickeners, like carrageen. Don't be concerned if when using homemade yogurt it seems to thin out more than dairy yogurt during the mixing of the ingredients. Your finished frozen yogurt will have the same fine texture and taste whichever type of yogurt—commercial or homemade—makes up the base.

A quart of dairy yogurt usually does not measure a full four cups. If a recipe calls for a quart, either add the extra yogurt, or use the quart of yogurt as is. There will be only little variation in the final results. When using homemade yogurt, measure the full four cups if indicated in the recipe.

EMULSIFIERS — An emulsifier must be added to the yogurt mixture before freezing. The emulsifier prevents formation of splintery ice crystals and smooths the yogurt during freezing into a creamy, fine-grained consistency. It also suspends fruit particles evenly throughout the mixture to give a balanced taste and texture. Unflavored gelatin, eggs, heavy cream and lecithin all are effective emulsifiers.

UNFLAVORED GELATIN — Unflavored gelatin is used most often in these recipes. It is convenient, is a natural product and contains few calories. One packet of gelatin equals the one tablespoon required in most recipes. Soften the gelatin in 1/4 cup water or juice, gently heat to dissolve, cool, and add to the yogurt mixture before freezing. One tablespoon of gelatin will emulsify about 4 to 7 cups of yogurt mixture. Gelatin slows down the rate at which frozen yogurt will melt when served.

EGGS — Eggs, as emulsifiers, produce an extremely fine-grained frozen yogurt. If you need to restrict your cholesterol intake, you may choose to use those recipes which do not contain egg yolk. Whipped egg whites folded into a yogurt mixture will help to emulsify and with fewer calories.

HEAVY CREAM — The high butterfat content of heavy cream makes it an excellent emulsifier. If calories and cholesterol are of no consequence to you, treat yourself to a *very* rich frozen yogurt with cream!

LECITHIN — Lecithin is a vegetable (soya) product which contains only polyunsaturated fat, no cholesterol. You can substitute liquid lecithin for gelatin for a similar emulsifying effect. The frozen yogurt will have an especially nice, creamy consistency. Exchange the lecithin in the proportion of *one teaspoon* for each one tablespoon of gelatin. A tablespoon of gelatin contains 25 calories, a teaspoon of lecithin contains 38 calories. Liquid lecithin is available at health food stores.

Since lecithin is a fat, it is difficult to disperse it evenly throughout a cold yogurt mixture. When using a recipe which combines ingredients in a blender, add the lecithin at that time. Or, if there is a honey to heat, warm the lecithin with the honey before adding to the yogurt mixture.

If, for dietary reasons, you choose to use nonfat yogurt in the recipes, you may want to substitute lecithin for gelatin as the emulsifier. The lecithin, as a fat, replaces the emulsifying butterfat found in whole milk or lowfat milk yogurt without the disadvantage of the cholesterol. When nonfat yogurt is the base of the yogurt mixture, lecithin smooths out the texture of the frozen yogurt better than gelatin.

SWEETENERS — Several options are available for sweetening the yogurt mixture before freezing. They include honey, light corn syrup, regular sugar and fructose. You may also want to try molasses, maple syrup or liquid brown sugar.

HONEY — Honey is the sweetener of choice for many people. It is a natural sweetener which contains none of the reputed disadvantages of refined sugars. If you use honey, choose a lightly-colored and mildly-flavored version. Otherwise your frozen yogurt will be dominated by a pronounced honey flavor which will prevent other flavors in the mixture from emerging fully. Honey sweetens more than sugar. Less honey is needed to achieve the same level of sweetness. Frozen yogurt made with honey can have fewer calories than frozen yogurt made with sugar.

CORN SYRUP — Corn syrup is useful in recipes when the flavor of honey is undesirable. It combines well with liquid ingredients. However, compared to sugar, a greater amount of corn syrup is needed to achieve the same level of sweetness—which means more calories. Corn syrup will sweeten, but it will not serve to highlight the subtle flavor nuances of fruit. For that effect you must use either regular sugar or fructose.

SUGAR — Sugar is the most familiar and the least expensive sweetener. Since it is highly refined, some people prefer to avoid its use. However, sugar does bring out peak fruit flavor more effectively than honey or corn syrup. It also counteracts the tang of yogurt more easily, if that is your desire.

FRUCTOSE — Fructose is the sugar which occurs naturally in fruits. It is extracted from such fruits as berries, pears, citrus fruits, cherries, apples and bananas. As a sweetener, fructose reacts excellently with fruit to accentuate vividly the nuances of the fruit flavor. Perhaps it is the best sweetener for this purpose. (Try it with boysenberries or raspberries—sensational!) Although fructose, too, is refined, it is preferred by many to regular cane sugar. It is chemically absorbed by the body differently and more slowly than other types of sugars. This is considered a health advantage by some.

Fructose is *very* sweet. When substituting fructose for sugar, you will need less. How much less depends upon your own taste preference. The calorie count is the same for a tablespoon of sugar or a tablespoon of fructose. If you can use less fructose for sweetening, you can lower the calories in your frozen yogurt.

The main problem with fructose is its cost. It is *very* expensive! Currently, fructose is not produced in large quantities and is occasionally difficult to find. Often, it can be located in health food stores or pharmacies. As information about fructose becomes more widely published, this sweetener should become more easily available. Hopefully, at a more reasonable price!

<u>FRUITS AND NUTS</u> — When pureed fruit is indicated in a recipe, don't completely liquify the fruit. If you use a blender, run it briefly and at a low speed. The fruit will then be liquified, but also pulpy. There will be small particles of fruit suspended throughout the frozen yogurt which will give it a more interesting texture and flavor.

To add nuts, coconut or marshmallows there are two methods which work out best. Fold them *very quickly* into the soft-frozen yogurt before popping it into the freezer to mellow. Or, add them to the yogurt mixture in the churn about 10 minutes after freezing has begun. Continue to freeze the mixture until done.

FREEZING THE YOGURT MIXTURE — The yogurt mixture can be frozen by using any one of several methods. Consistency and density of the frozen yogurt will vary slightly depending upon the freezing method used and the amount of air churned into the yogurt. Some yogurt mixtures are quite dense. Expect those to expand less than ice cream during the freezing process. For convenience, you can blend your yogurt mixture ahead and chill it for several hours or overnight before freezing.

ICE CREAM FREEZERS (Electric or Hand-cranked) — These familiar ice cream freezers make the best quality homemade frozen yogurt. The dasher continuously blends air into the mixture, which prevents the formation of ice crystals. A very creamy, fine-grained frozen yogurt results, with the consistency of soft-frozen ice cream.

Essentially, this method is the same as for ice cream. The mixture is churned until softly frozen, the dasher is removed, and the frozen yogurt is ripened or mellowed for a few hours in the canister of the ice cream freezer or in the home freezer. However, the ice cream freezers do vary widely in their efficiency. Those with wooden buckets tend to insulate the rock salt and ice best and maintain the most consistent level of coldness. This allows the mixture to freeze smoothly and fully. Those freezers with plastic buckets, while satisfactory, do not insulate as well and sometimes fail to freeze the yogurt as fully. If this happens to your frozen yogurt, when the machine has stopped place the canister immediately in the freezer compartment of your refrigerator. After about an hour, pack it into containers for further mellowing or storage. Follow the instructions which accompany your particular ice cream freezer for specific method and ice-salt proportions. All recipes may be doubled or tripled for the larger capacities of these freezing units.

IN-FREEZER ICE CREAM FREEZERS — These electrical units churn within the freezer portion of the refrigerator, without the need for ice or salt. They perform well only inside of a home freezer which maintains 0°F. If your freezer is warmer—for instance, on a very hot day—the yogurt mixture will not freeze properly. This type of ice cream freezer makes one quart of frozen yogurt. Put no more than about 3-1/3 cups of unfrozen yogurt mixture into the canister to allow room for expansion during the churning. Most recipes here can be halved for use with these units. Either leave the gelatin in the recipe at 1 tablespoon for a more custardy frozen yogurt, or decrease the gelatin by half along with the rest of the ingredients. If you retain the whole tablespoon of gelatin in the recipe, do not pre-chill the mixture before freezing. It will congeal and become quite thick and then overtax the motor of the ice cream freezer. These small motors do not have enough power to churn through heavy gelatinized mixtures and will burn out.

FREEZER TRAYS — If you have neither type of ice cream freezer, don't despair! You can still make homemade frozen yogurt! Pour the yogurt mixture into freezer trays (ice trays) and set them in the freezer compartment of your refrigerator. When about an inch of freezing has occurred around the inside edges of the trays, put the semi-frozen mixture into a chilled mixing bowl (metal keeps it colder). Whip it quickly with an electric mixer to break up the ice crystals. Return the yogurt to the trays. Continue freezing. Repeat this two or three times while the yogurt is freezing for a smoother frozen yogurt.

SERVING FROZEN YOGURT — When first frozen in the ice cream freezer, your frozen yogurt will have the consistency of commercial soft-frozen yogurt. If you prefer this softer, creamier version, by all means serve it immediately! Or, mellow the soft-frozen yogurt in the ice cream canister or in your freezer for two or three hours to improve the flavor.

As with hard-frozen ice cream, yogurt which has been stored in the freezer should be removed for a few minutes before serving to thaw to the desired consistency.

STORING FROZEN YOGURT — When packing frozen yogurt into containers for mellowing or storing in the freezer, pack it somewhat loosely—and *quickly!* Frozen yogurt will keep for several weeks in the freezer. Some of the bacteria in the yogurt will be destroyed gradually by the prolonged freezing. If viability of the bacteria is important to you, the solution is simple—eat your frozen yogurt desserts within a few days!

FRUIT FROZEN YOGURT — BASIC RECIPE

2 cups pureed fresh,
    frozen or canned fruit
1/2 to 3/4 cup sugar

1 tbs. unflavored gelatin
1/4 cup water or juice
1 qt. yogurt

Puree fruit in blender. Add sugar. Set aside for 1/2 hour. Soften gelatin in water. Warm gently over low heat until dissolved. Cool. Combine fruit mixture, gelatin and yogurt. Freeze (see page 163). Makes about 2 quarts.

STRAWBERRY FROZEN YOGURT — Use 2 cups pureed fresh or frozen strawberries and add 2 tablespoons vanilla extract to basic recipe. Optional— fold in 1 cup mini-marshmallows, chopped banana or crushed pineapple.

BOYSENBERRY OR BLACKBERRY FROZEN YOGURT — Use 1 cup pureed berries, and add 1 tablespoon vanilla extract to basic recipe.

CHERRY FROZEN YOGURT — Use 2 cups *chopped* fresh bing cherries, and add 1/4 teaspoon almond extract to basic recipe.

FRUIT FROZEN YOGURT

Mix and freeze as directed in basic recipe on page 167.

BANANA FROZEN YOGURT — 1 tablespoon gelatin, 1/4 cup water, 4 tablespoons honey (heat with gelatin to melt), 2 cups mashed bananas mixed with 1 tablespoon lemon juice, 1 quart yogurt, 1 tablespoon vanilla extract. Makes about 2 quarts. Optional—add 1 cup mini-marshmallows, chocolate bits or nuts.

PEACH FROZEN YOGURT — 2 cups pureed fresh peaches mixed with 1/2 cup sugar and 1 tablespoon lemon juice. Use 1 tablespoon gelatin, 1/4 cup water, 3 cups yogurt, 1 tablespoon vanilla extract and 1/4 teaspoon almond extract. Makes about 1-3/4 quarts.

CARAMEL-NECTARINE FROZEN YOGURT — 2 cups pureed nectarines mixed with 1 cup brown sugar and 1 tablespoon lemon juice. Use 1 tablespoon gelatin, 1/4 cup water, 1 quart yogurt, 1 tablespoon vanilla extract, 1 tablespoon Mapleine, 1 teaspoon cinnamon, 1/4 teaspoon freshly-grated nutmeg and 1 cup chopped pecans. Makes about 2 quarts.

CRANBERRY-NUT FROZEN YOGURT — 2 cups fresh cranberries, chopped, mixed with 1 cup sugar and 1 teaspoon cinnamon. Use 1 tablespoon gelatin, 1/4 cup orange juice, 1 quart yogurt and 1/2 cup chopped walnuts. Makes about 2 quarts.

APPLE-CINNAMON FROZEN YOGURT — 1 tablespoon gelatin, 1/4 cup apple juice, 6 tablespoons honey (heat with gelatin to melt), 2 cups unsweetened applesauce, 1 quart yogurt, 1 teaspoon cinnamon. Makes about 2 quarts. Top with whipped cream and grated cheddar cheese.

MINCEMEAT FROZEN YOGURT — 1 tablespoon gelatin, 1/4 cup orange juice, 1-1/2 to 2 cups canned or homemade mincemeat, 1 quart yogurt. Makes about 1-3/4 to 2 quarts.

STRAWBERRY-ORANGE FROZEN YOGURT — 2 cups pureed strawberries mixed with 1/2 cup sugar. Use 1 tablespoon gelatin, 1/4 cup water, 2 cups yogurt, 1 tablespoon vanilla extract and 1/4 cup orange liqueur. Makes about 1-1/3 quarts.

FRUIT FROZEN YOGURT continued

RUMPOT MELANGE FROZEN YOGURT — If you have a rumpot going, use 2 cups coarsely-chopped marinated fruit. Soften and dissolve 1 tablespoon gelatin in 1/2 cup of the rumpot syrup. Use 1 quart yogurt. This frozen yogurt is different each time it is made, depending upon the seasonal fruits used in the rumpot.

AVOCADO-HONEY FROZEN YOGURT — 2 cups mashed, ripe avocado mixed with 2 to 3 tablespoons fresh lime juice and 1/4 teaspoon salt. Use 1 tablespoon gelatin, 1/2 cup pineapple juice, 1/2 cup honey (heat with gelatin to melt), 3 cups yogurt and 1/4 teaspoon grated lime zest. Combine in blender. Makes about 1-3/4 quarts. Serve topped with toasted coconut.

PAPAYA-PINEAPPLE FROZEN YOGURT — 1 tablespoon gelatin, 1/3 cup pineapple juice, 1/4 cup honey (heat with gelatin to melt), 2 cups mashed papaya, 1 tablespoon fresh lime juice, 3 cups yogurt, 1 tablespoon vanilla extract, 1/2 teaspoon grated lime zest and 3/4 cup drained, crushed pineapple. Makes about 2 quarts. Serve topped with shredded coconut.

FIG-WALNUT FROZEN YOGURT — Poach 2-1/2 cups sliced fresh figs with 1/4 cup apple juice, 1/4 cup water and 6 tablespoons honey for 10 minutes. Chop fruit. Cool. Soften and dissolve 1 tablespoon gelatin in 1/4 cup cooled fig liquid. Combine figs and remaining liquid, gelatin, 2 cups yogurt, 1 teaspoon vanilla extract and 1 cup chopped walnuts. Makes about 1-1/2 quarts.

GUAVA FROZEN YOGURT — Poach 4 cups peeled and sliced guavas with 1/2 cup water, 1 cup sugar and 1 tablespoon lemon juice for 10 minutes. Chop fruit. Cool. Soften and dissolve 1 tablespoon gelatin in 1/4 cup cooled guava liquid. Combine guavas and remaining liquid, gelatin, 3 cups yogurt, 2 teaspoons vanilla extract and 1/4 teaspoon cinnamon. (Use mixture of ripe and semi-ripe guavas.) Makes about 2 quarts.

DATE-PECAN FROZEN YOGURT — Pit and quarter 1 package (16 ozs.) dried natural dates. Whirl in blender with 1-1/2 cups warm water and 1/2 cup brown sugar until pureed. Use 1 tablespoon gelatin, 1/4 cup water, 2 cups yogurt and 1 cup chopped pecans. Makes about 1-3/4 quarts.

FRUIT JUICE FROZEN YOGURT — BASIC RECIPE

Use any frozen fruit juice concentrate—grape, orange, cranberry, apple, tangerine, pineapple, lemonade, grapefruit, daiquiri, or orange-pineapple.

1 can (6 ozs.) frozen juice concentrate	1/4 cup water
1 tbs. unflavored gelatin	1 qt. yogurt

Defrost juice. Soften gelatin in water. Dissolve over low heat. Cool. Mix with juice and yogurt. Sweeten to taste. Freeze (see page 163). Makes about 1-1/2 quarts.

ORANGE-HONEY FROZEN YOGURT — Use orange concentrate. Melt 1/2 cup honey with gelatin, and add 2 teaspoons grated orange zest.

PINEAPPLE-DAIQUIRI FROZEN YOGURT — Use daiquiri concentrate, 1 tablespoon gelatin, 1/3 cup pineapple juice, 3/4 cup sugar, 1 quart yogurt, 3 tablespoons rum, 1 tablespoon vanilla extract and 1-1/2 cups drained, crushed pineapple. Variation—Omit pineapple. Substitute bananas, strawberries or papaya.

HONEY VANILLA FROZEN YOGURT

1/2 cup honey
1 cup heavy cream
3 tbs. vanilla
3 cups yogurt

Gently heat honey to melt. Cool. Whip cream. Combine honey, vanilla and yogurt. Fold in whipped cream. Freeze (see page 163). Makes about 1 quart.

VARIATIONS — Fold in one of the following—fresh raspberries or blueberries, toasted nuts or coconut, crushed peanut brittle, semi-sweet chocolate, carob or butterscotch bits, crumbled coconut macaroons soaked in brandy or rum. Swirl in jam, chocolate sauce, syrup, dessert topping or liqueur—creme de menthe, orange, coffee, pistachio, apricot, almond, plum, etc.

VANILLA CUSTARD FROZEN YOGURT

6 egg yolks, lightly beaten   1/4 tsp. salt
2 cups half and half   3 tbs. vanilla extract
1-1/2 cups sugar   3 cups yogurt

Combine egg yolks, cream, sugar and salt in top of double boiler. Cook, stirring, over hot water until mixture becomes slightly thickened and lightly coats spoon. Strain. Add vanilla. Chill. Mix yogurt and chilled custard. Freeze (see page 163). Makes about 2 quarts.

LEMON CUSTARD FROZEN YOGURT — Before freezing fold in 1/3 cup lemon or lime juice and 2 tablespoons grated lemon or lime zest. Optional—fold in 1 cup shredded coconut.

CHOCOLATE CUSTARD FROZEN YOGURT — Add 2 ounces unsweetened chocolate to custard mixture before cooking.

SWEET CHOCOLATE FROZEN YOGURT

1 tbs. unflavored gelatin
1 cup heavy cream
1-1/4 cups sugar
2 ozs. unsweetened chocolate
2 cups yogurt
1 tbs. vanilla

In saucepan, soften gelatin in cream. Add sugar and chocolate. Heat, stirring, until sugar has dissolved and chocolate melted. Cool. Beat with electric mixer or hand beater. Combine chocolate, yogurt and vanilla. Freeze (see page 163). Makes about 1 quart.

VARIATION — For a tangier chocolate, decrease sugar 1/4 cup and increase yogurt 1 cup.

ROCKY ROAD FROZEN YOGURT — Fold 3/4 cup lightly-toasted slivered almonds and 1 cup mini-marshmallows into soft-frozen yogurt before mellowing.

CHOCOLATE-CHERRY FROZEN YOGURT — Fold 1 can (21 ozs.) cherry pie filling into yogurt mixture before freezing.

CHOCOLATE-ORANGE FROZEN YOGURT — Add 4 tablespoons orange liqueur and 1 tablespoon grated orange zest to yogurt mixture before freezing.

PEANUT BUTTER-MAPLE FROZEN YOGURT

Serve this for breakfast with sliced bananas and sprinkled with granola. Children love it, and it's an easy, nourishing way to start the day! This is also a perfect after-school energy snack—filled with protein!

1 tbs. unflavored gelatin
1/4 cup apple juice
1/2 cup firmly-packed brown sugar
1/2 cup honey

2 tsp. Mapleine
2 cups chunky-style peanut
    butter (room temperature)
4 cups yogurt

Soften gelatin in apple juice. Heat gently to dissolve. Add sugar. Heat, stirring, until dissolved. Cool. Mix honey and Mapleine into peanut butter. Combine gelatin mixture, peanut butter and yogurt. Freeze (see page 163). Makes about 2 quarts.

VARIATIONS — Fold in 1 cup semi-sweet chocolate or carob chips, or alternate layers of soft-frozen yogurt with jam or chocolate sauce before mellowing.

EXTRA-RICH FROZEN YOGURT

HOLIDAY EGGNOG FROZEN YOGURT — 1 quart fresh dairy eggnog, 1 quart yogurt and 3 tablespoons rum. Freeze. Makes about 2-1/2 quarts. Top with whipped cream. Dust with freshly-grated nutmeg.

TOASTED ALMOND FROZEN YOGURT — 1 tablespoon gelatin, 1/4 cup water, 3 cups yogurt, 1 cup heavy cream, 1/2 cup sugar, 2 tablespoons vanilla extract, 2 to 3 tablespoons sherry, 3/4 teaspoon almond extract, 1 cup toasted almonds.

COCONUT CREAM FROZEN YOGURT — 1 tablespoon gelatin, 1/4 cup water, 1 can (16 ozs.) Kern's Cream of Coconut (don't substitute other brands), 3 cups yogurt. Makes about 1-1/2 quarts. Variations—Fold in 1 cup chocolate bits or chopped pecans. Swirl jam or chocolate sauce into soft-frozen yogurt before mellowing. Fold in toasted coconut, top with Kahlua.

COCONUT AMBROSIA FROZEN YOGURT — Add 3/4 cup drained, crushed pinapple to coconut cream mixture. When soft-frozen, fold in 3/4 cup chopped pecans, 3/4 cup coconut, and 1/2 cup chopped maraschino cherries.

INDEX